This book belongs to....

....

....

Small preview of what's inside

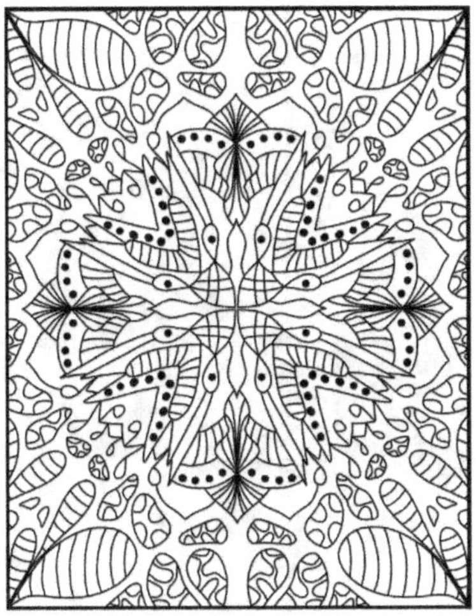

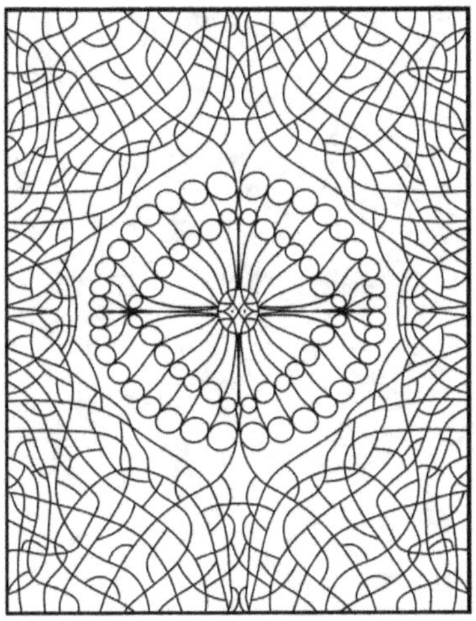

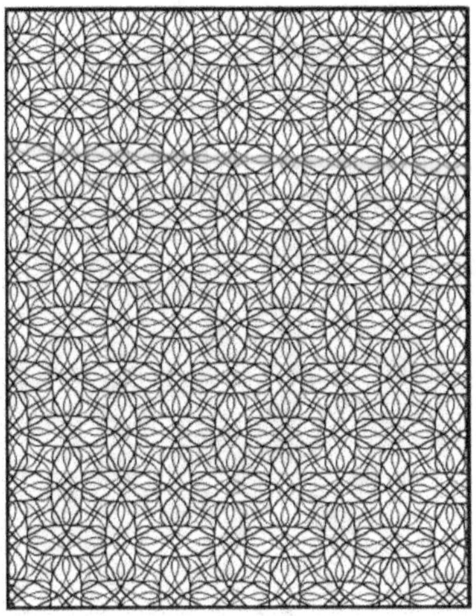

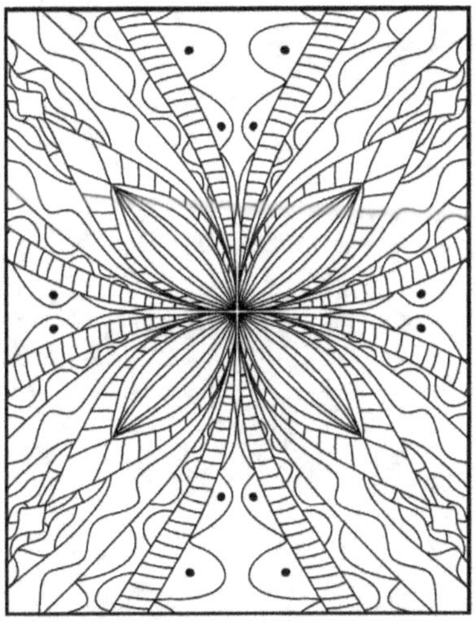

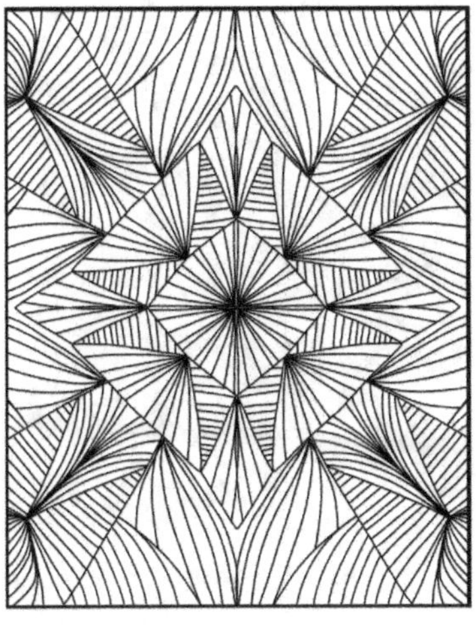

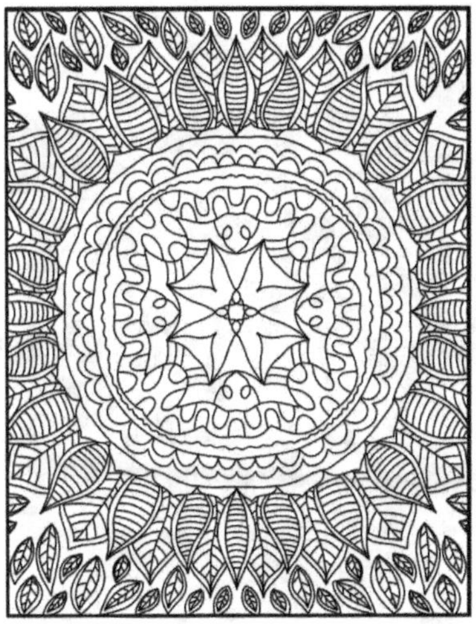

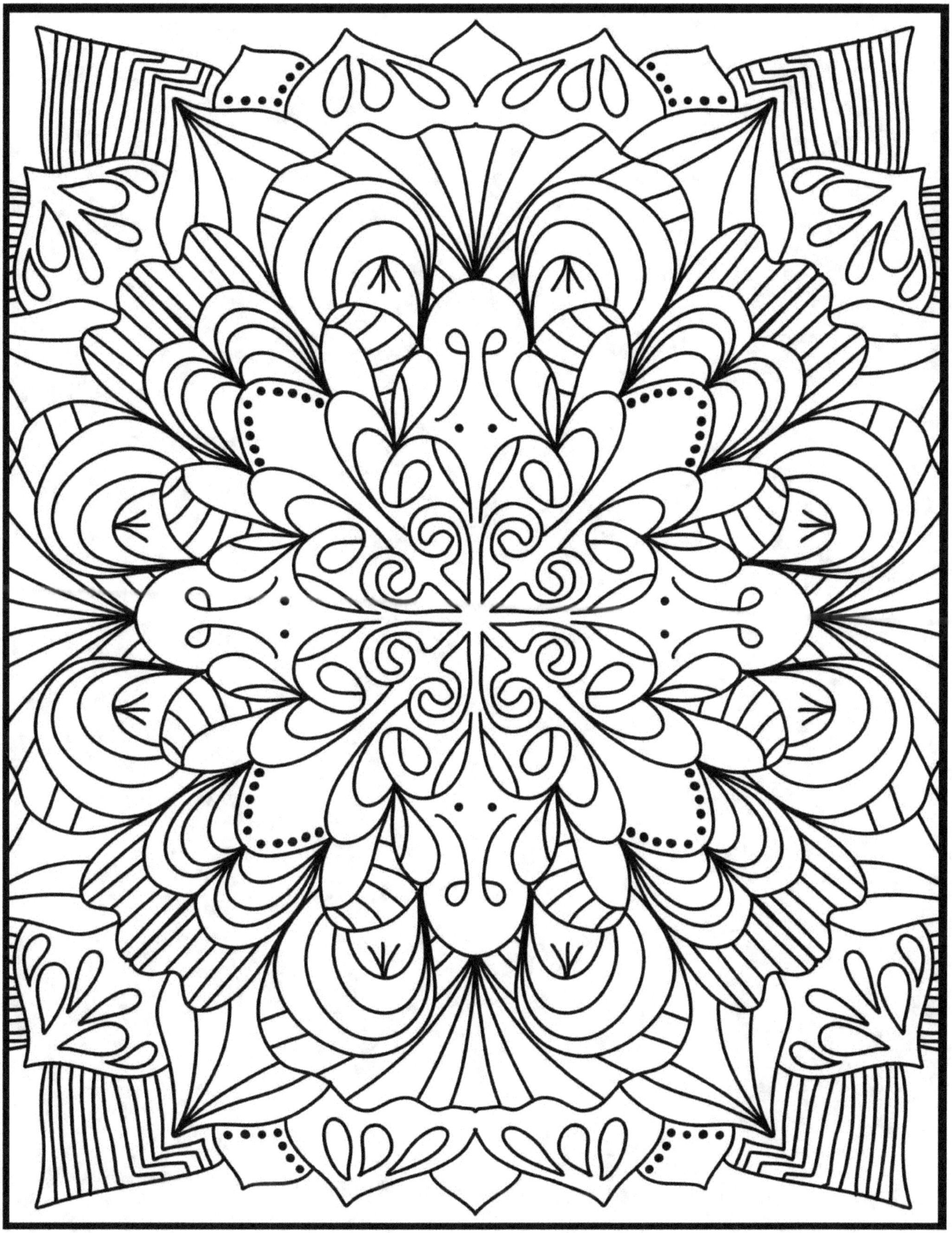

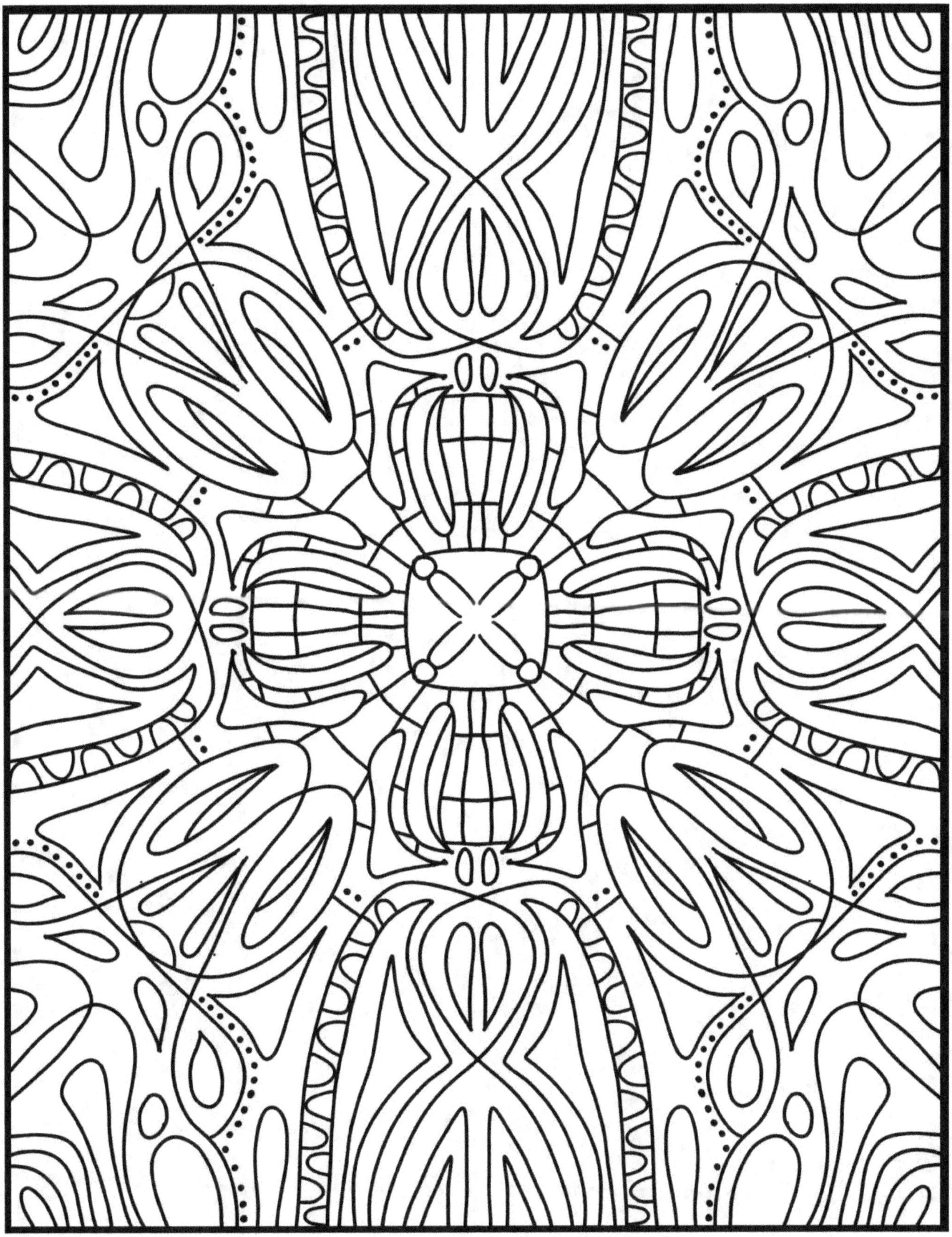

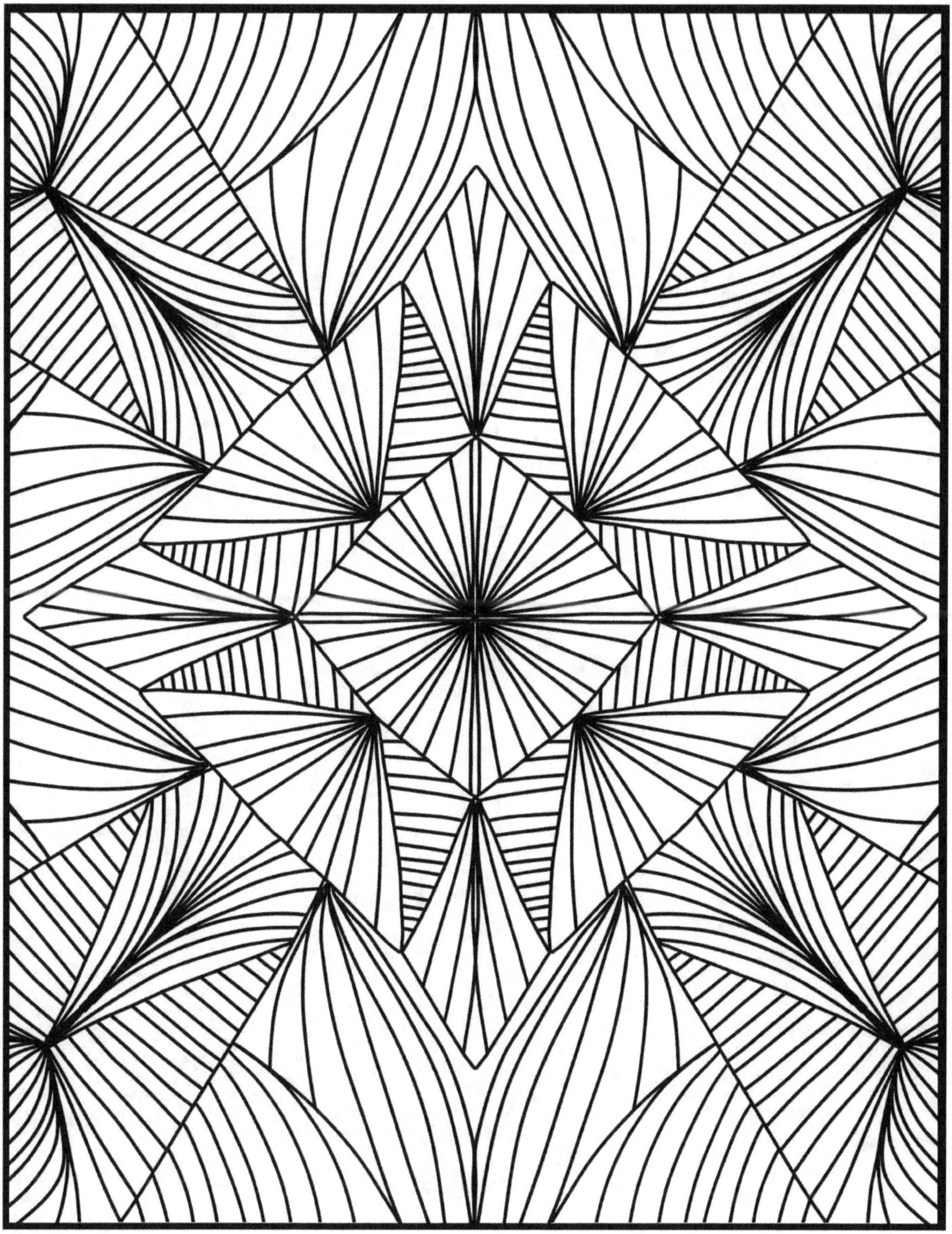

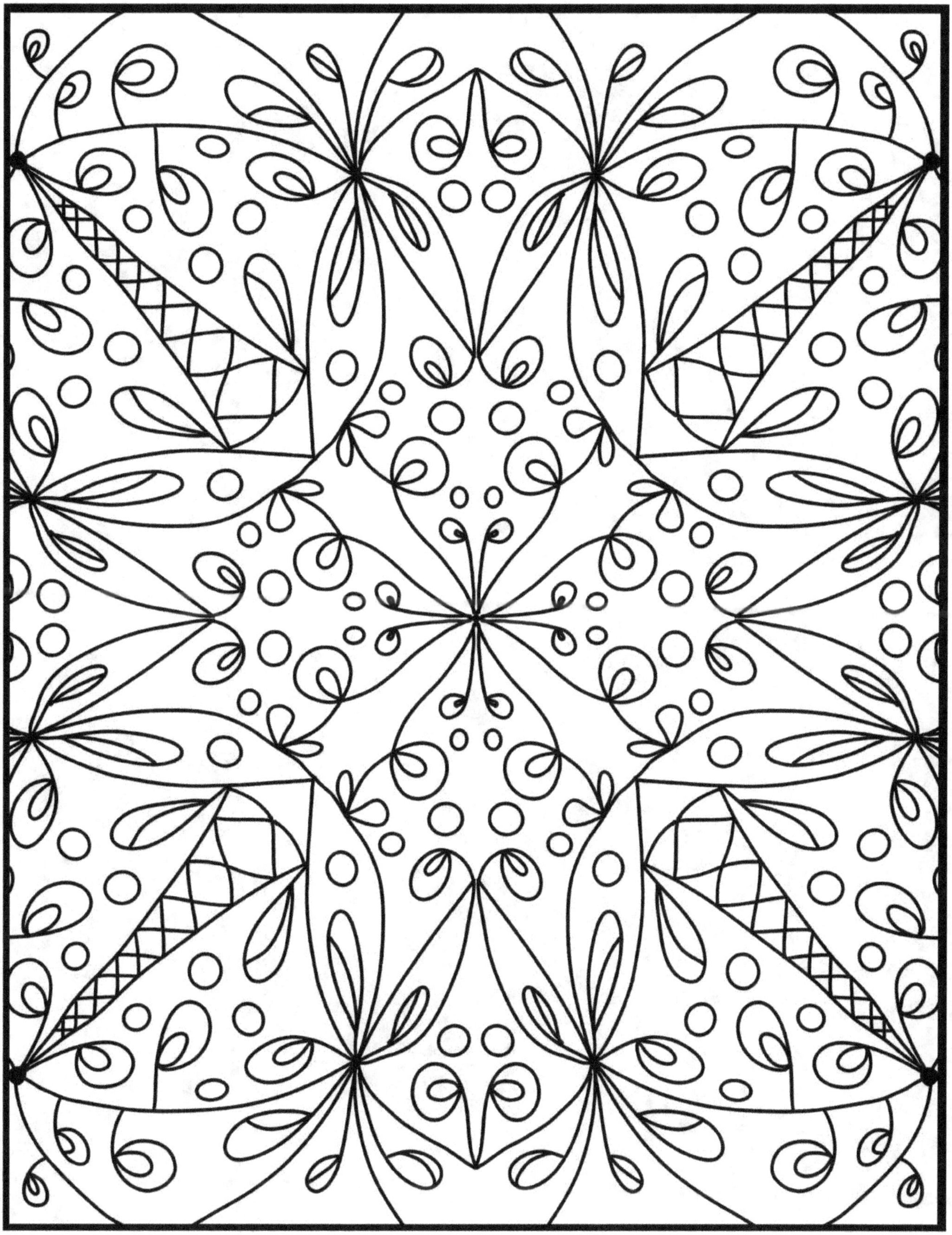

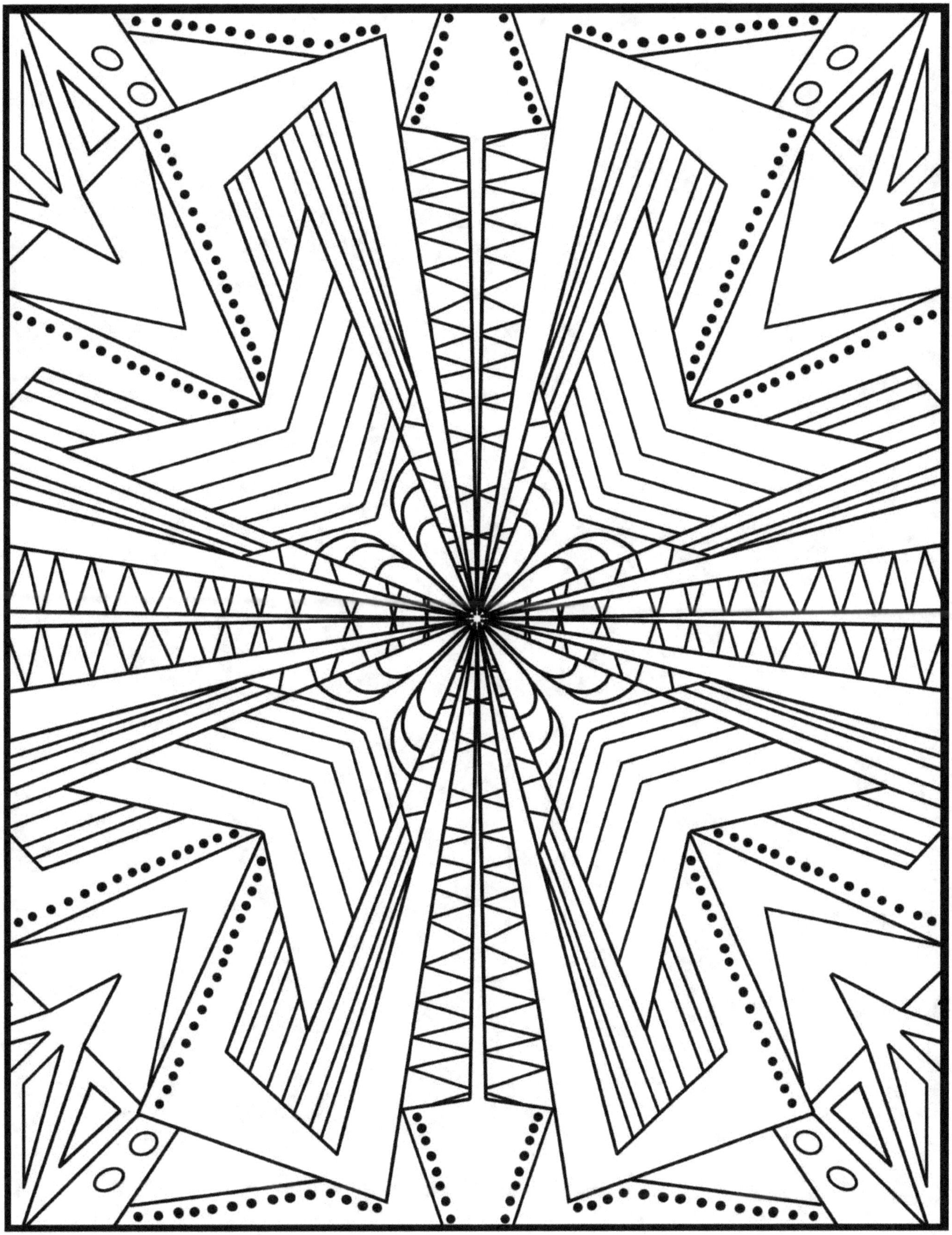

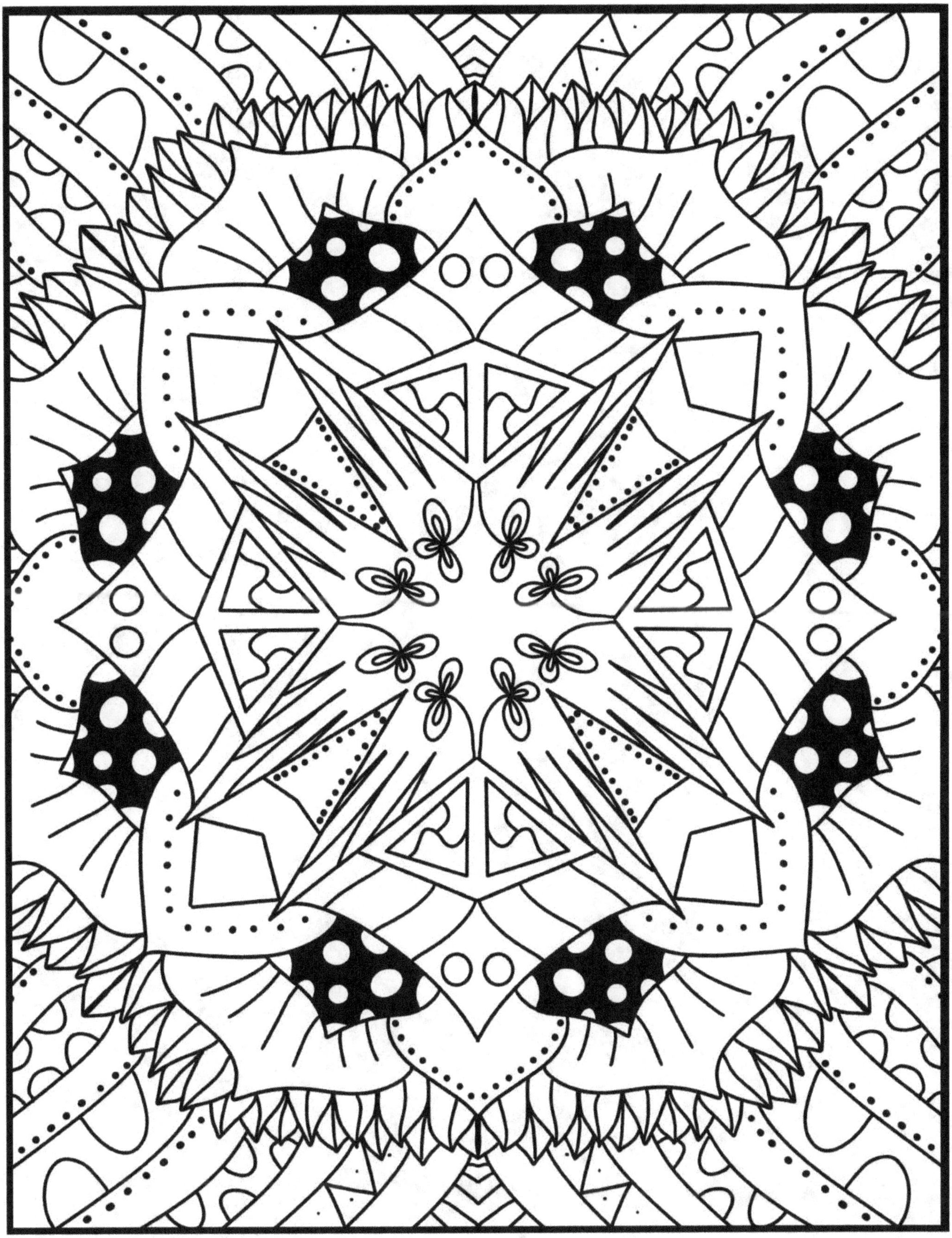

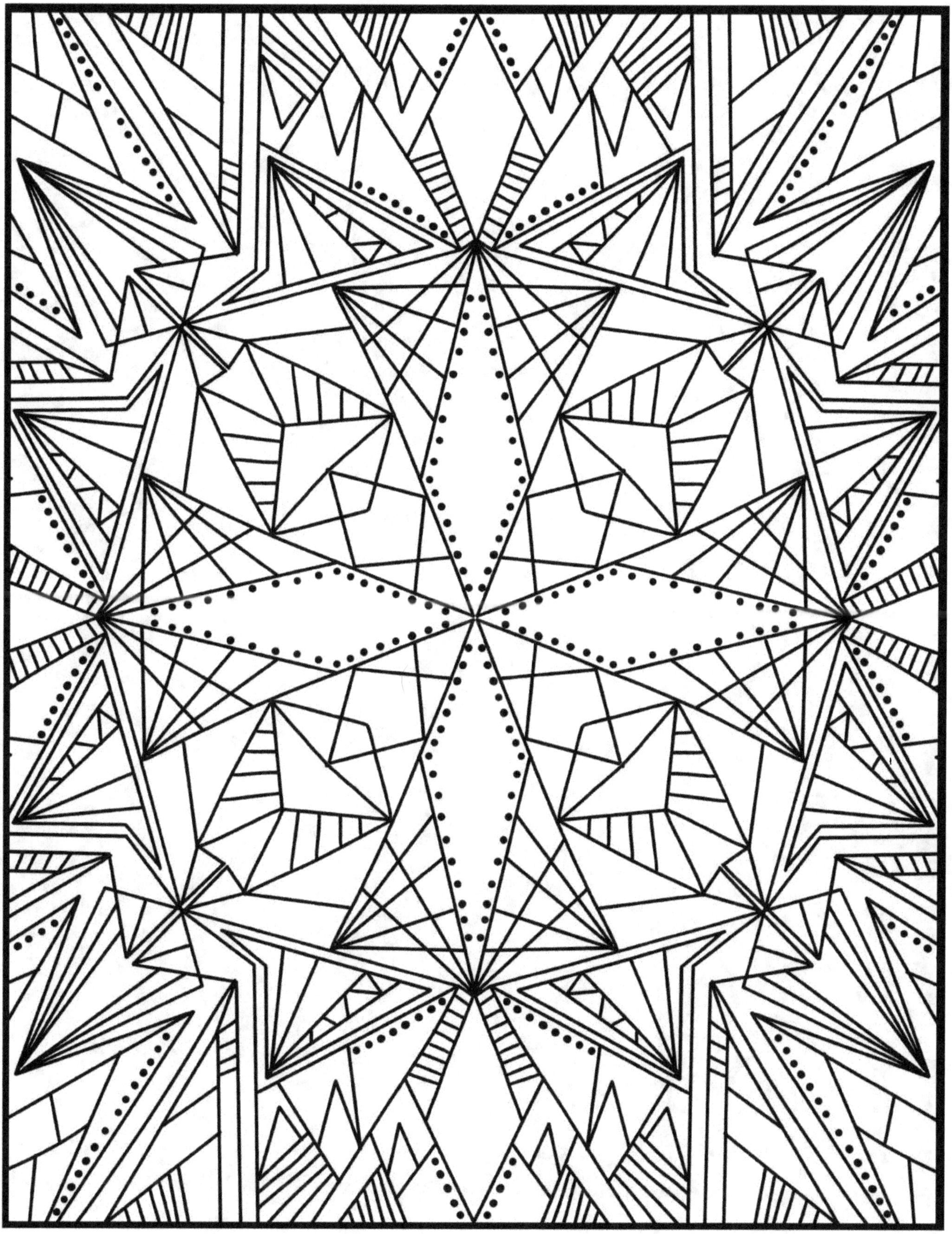

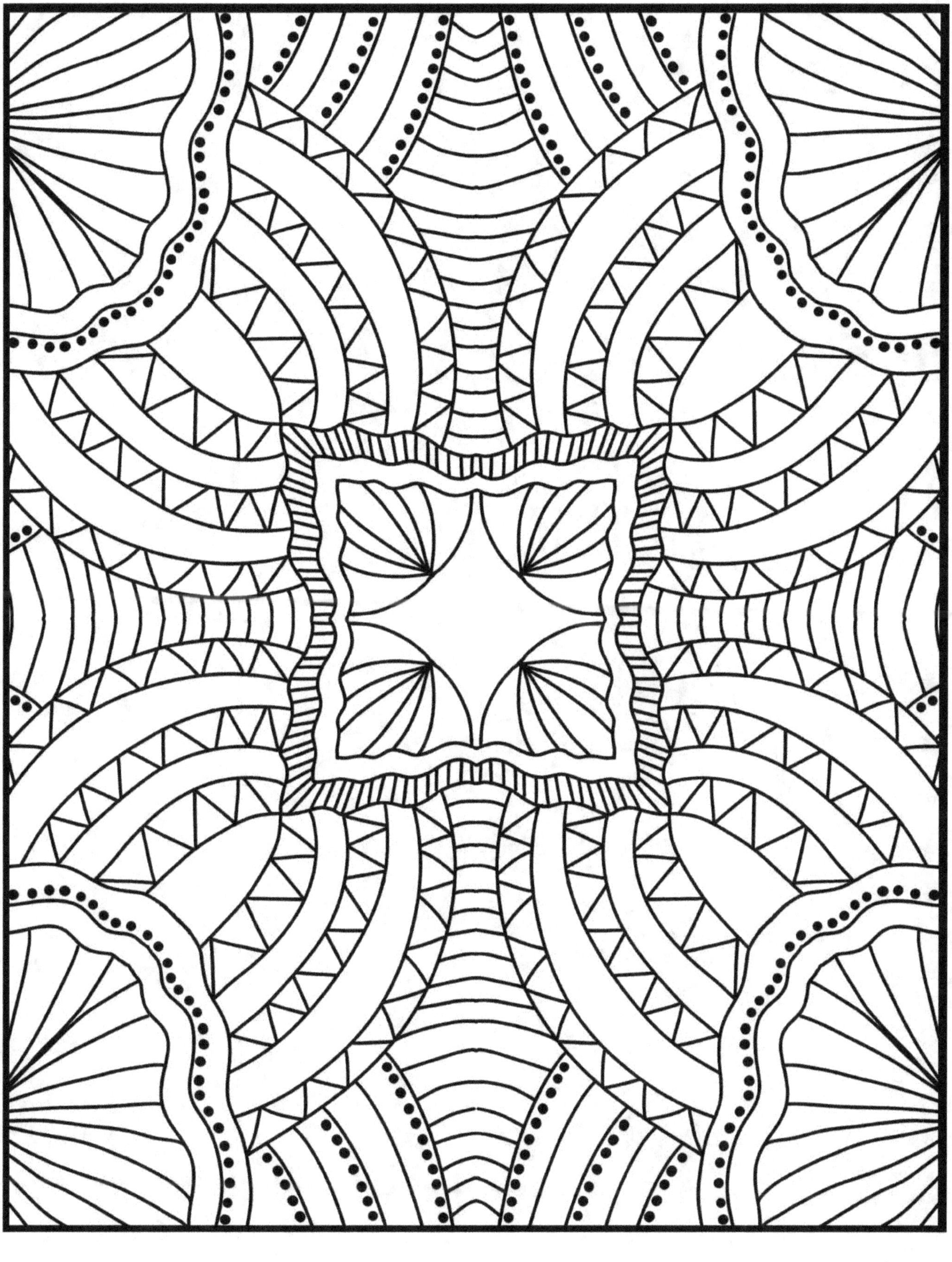

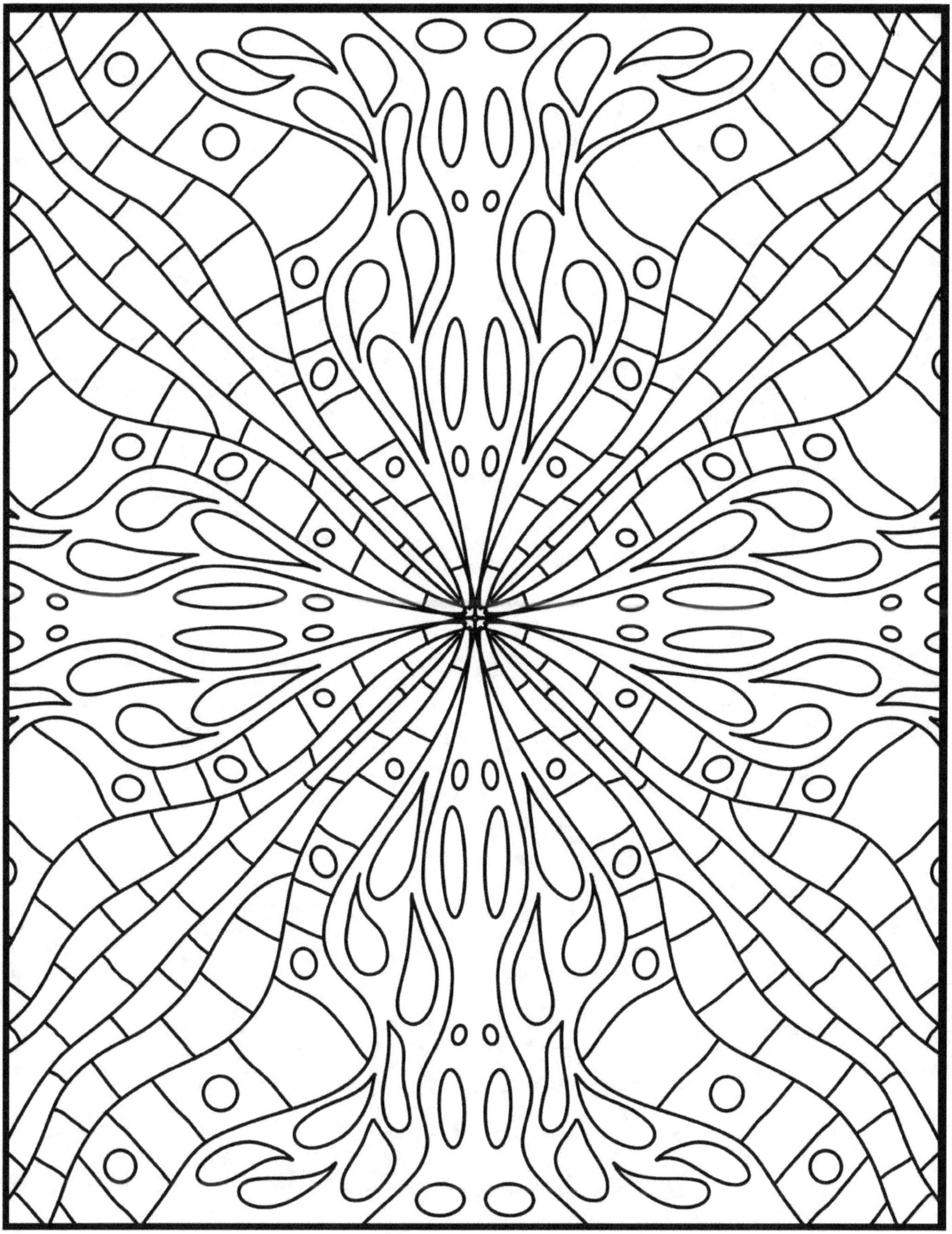

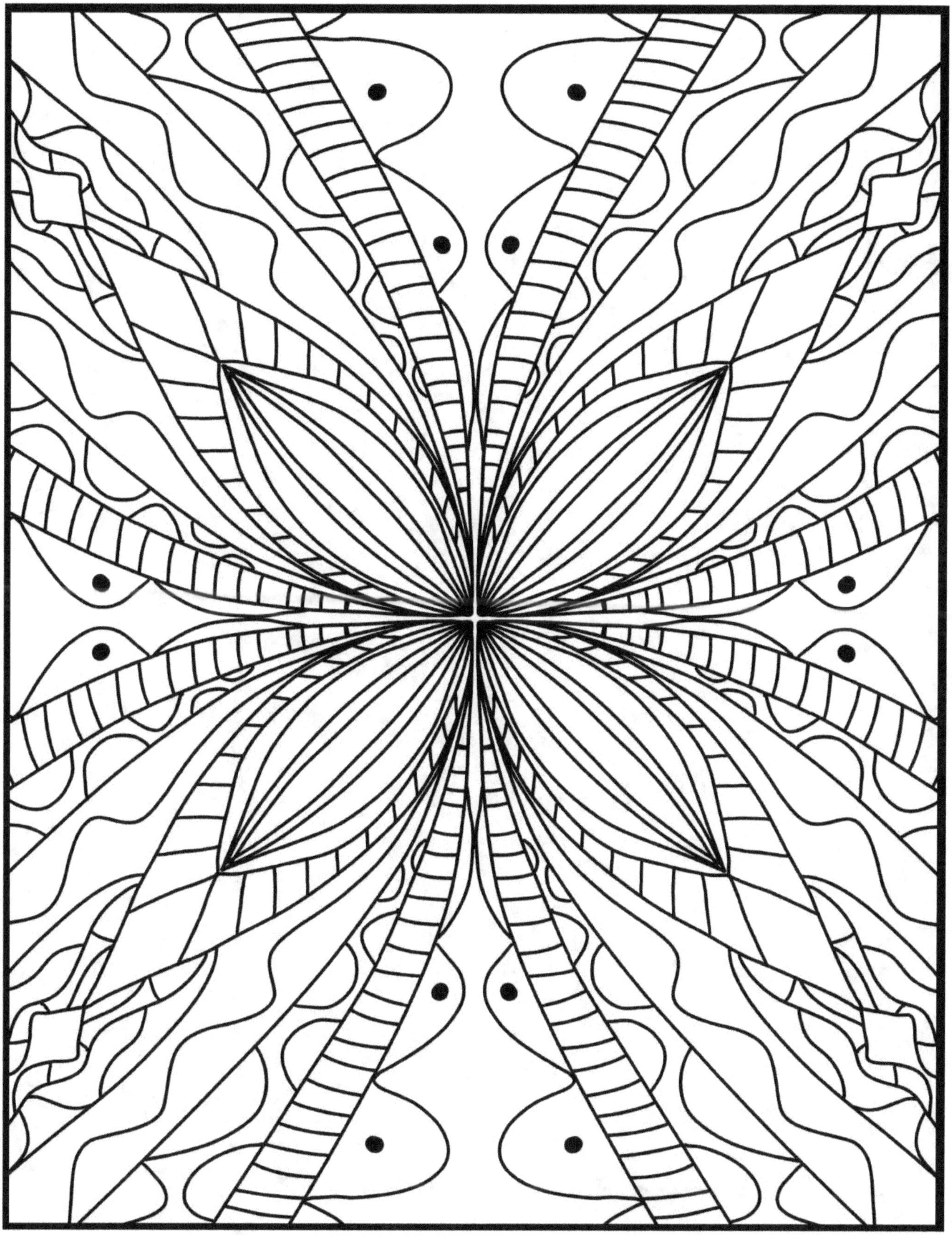

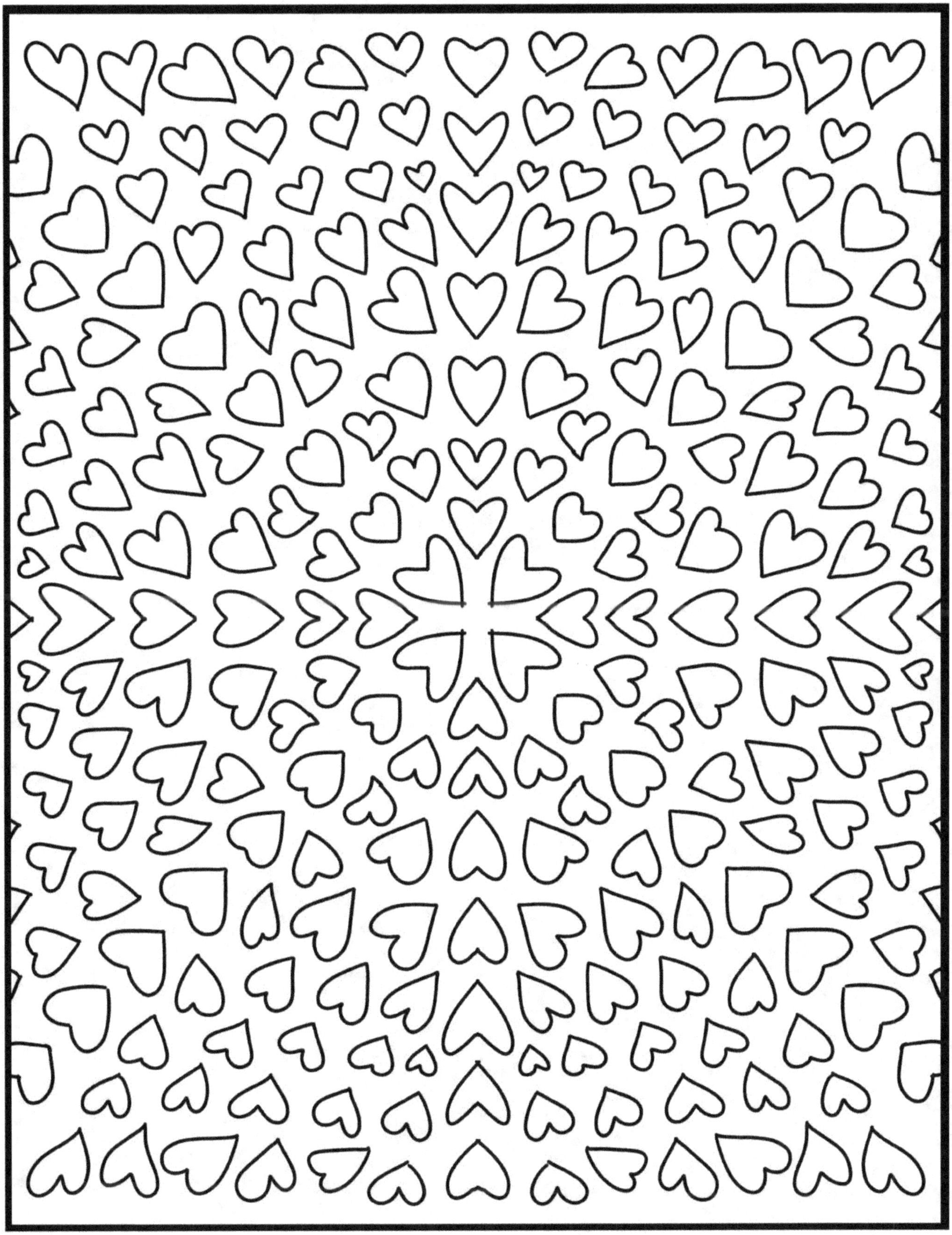

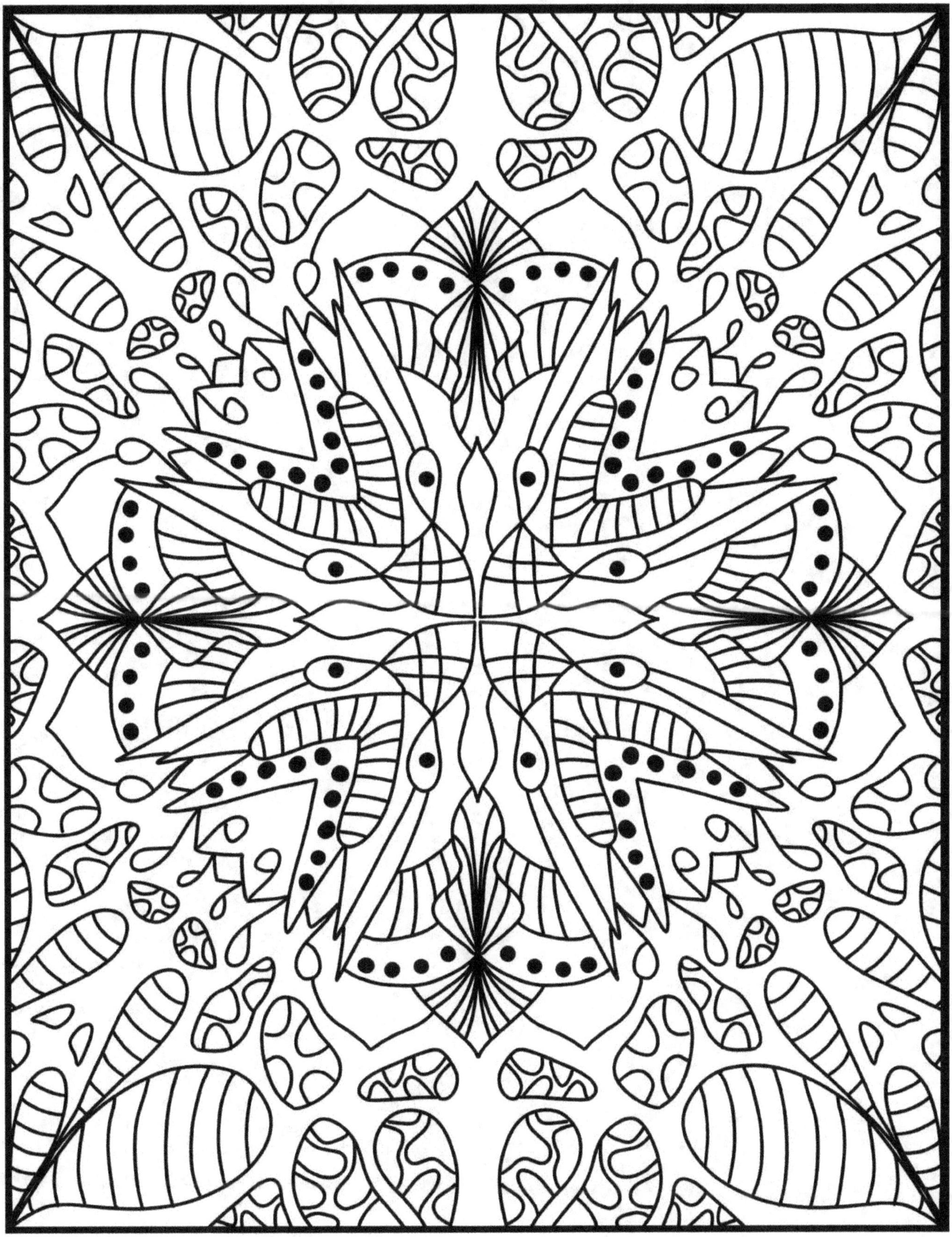

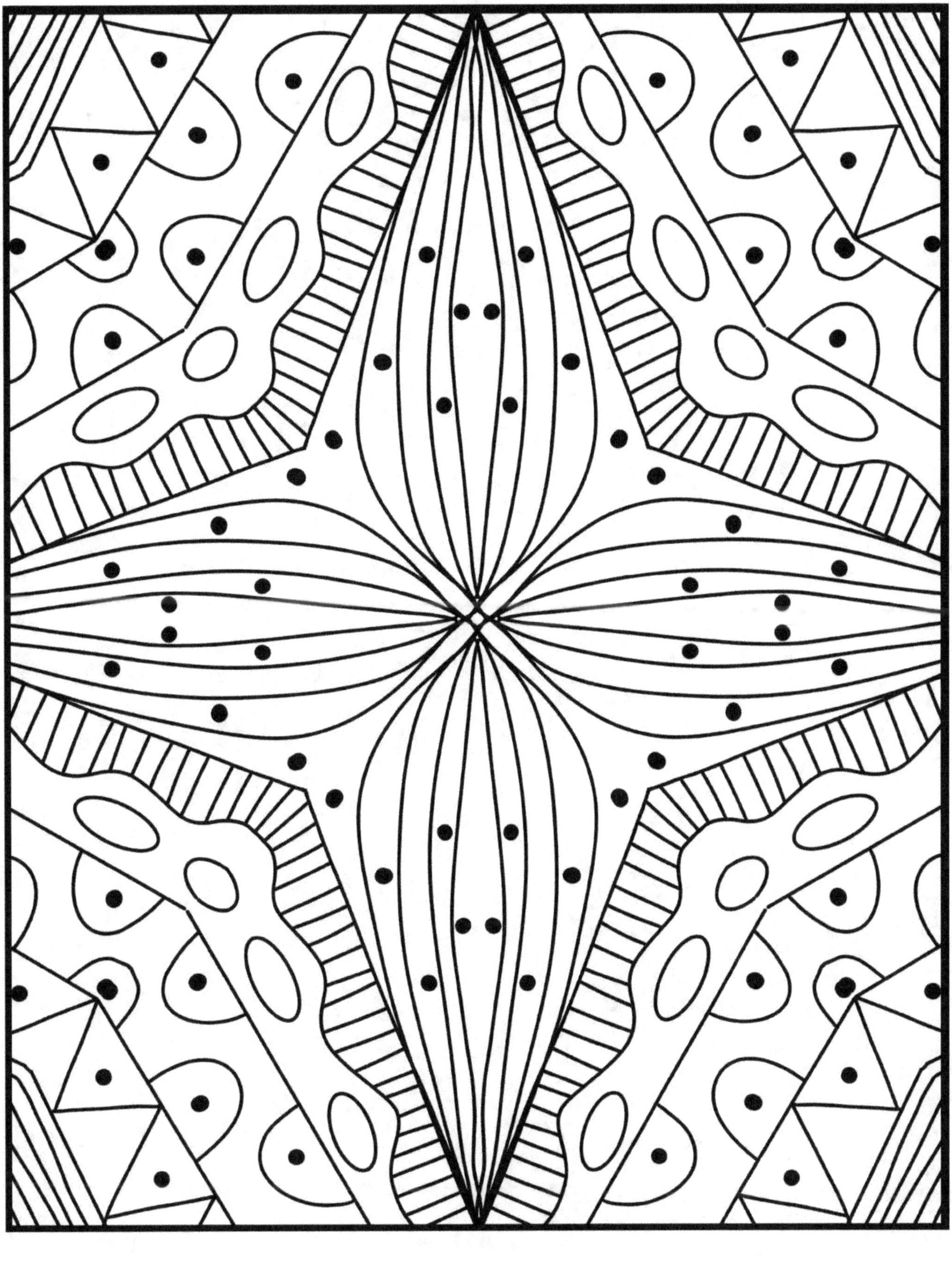

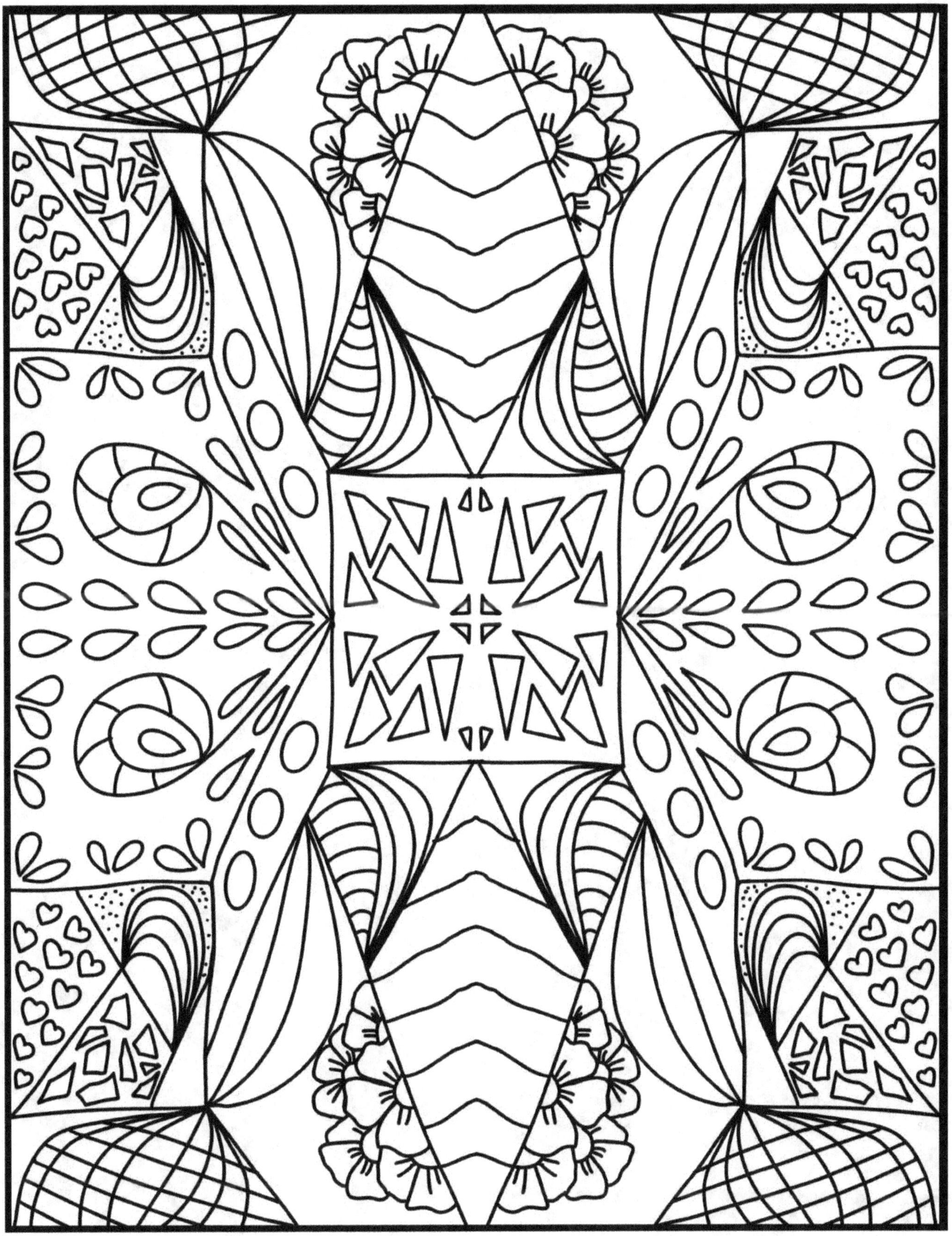

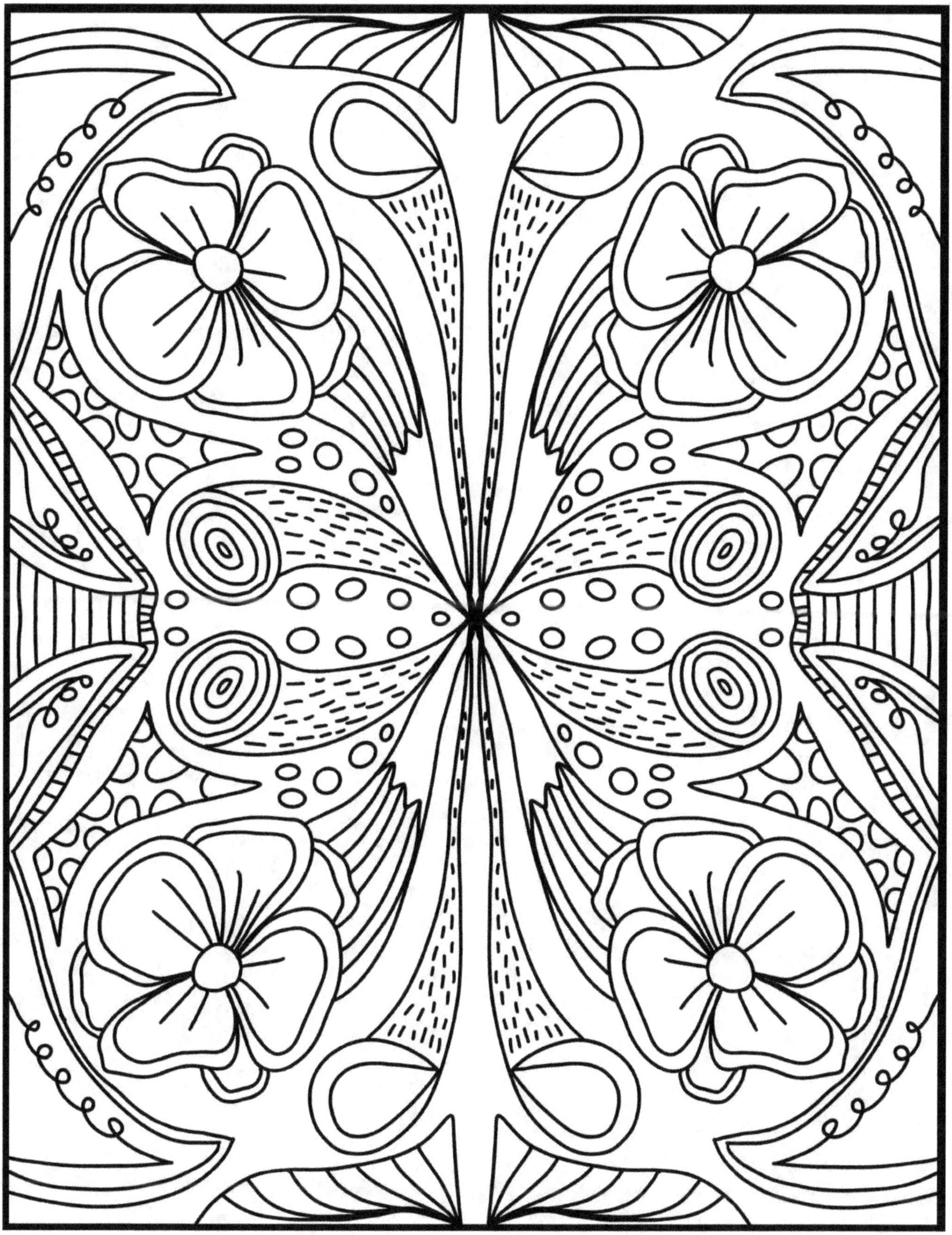

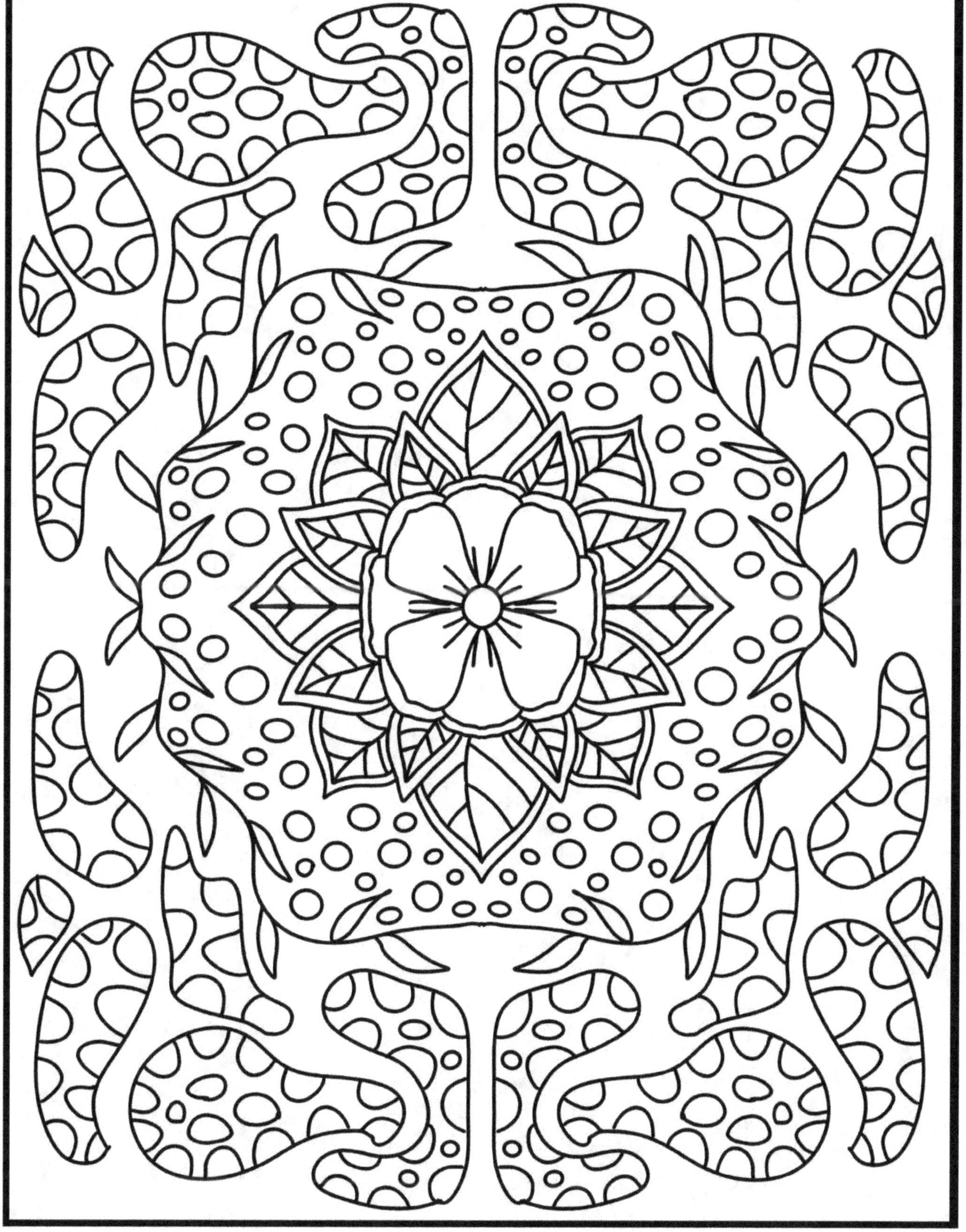

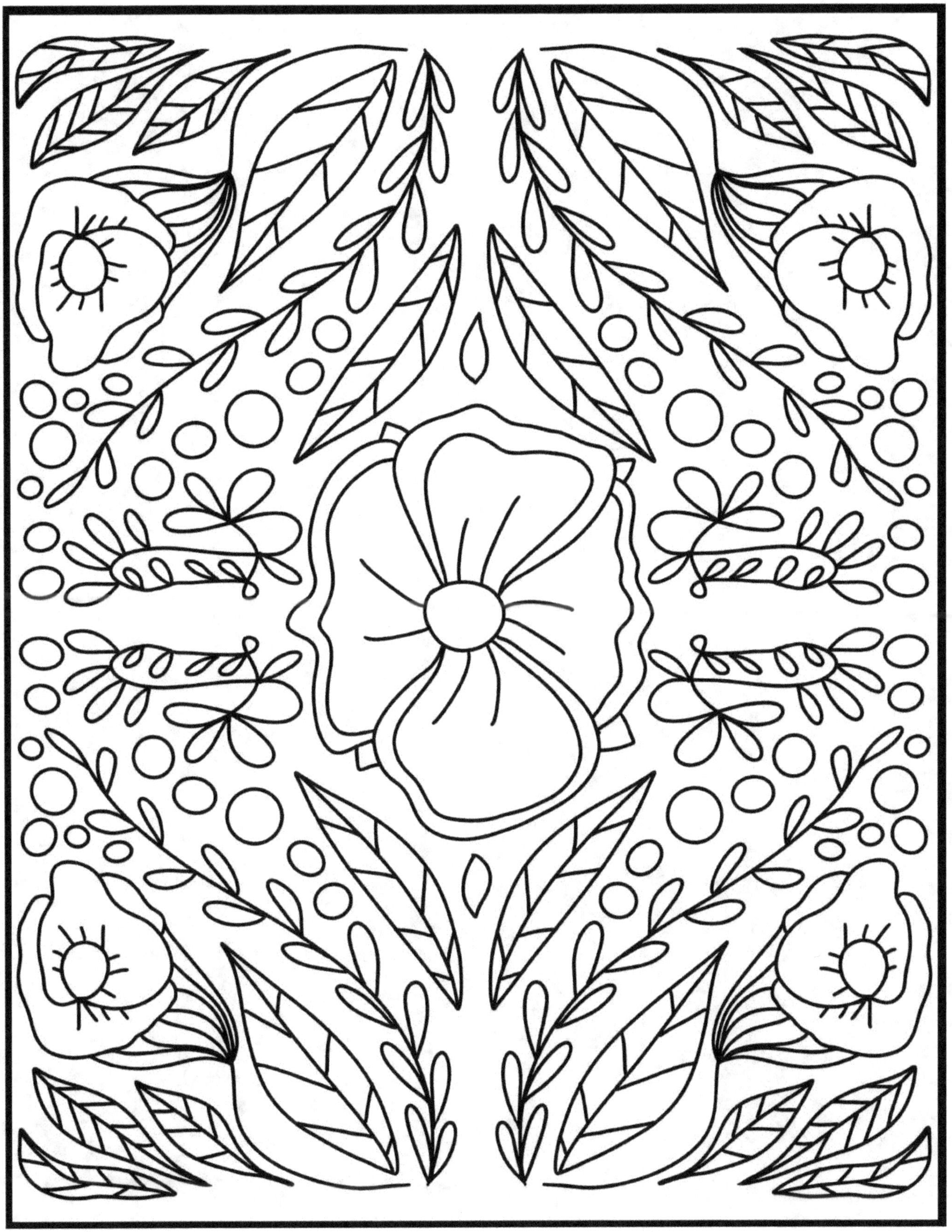

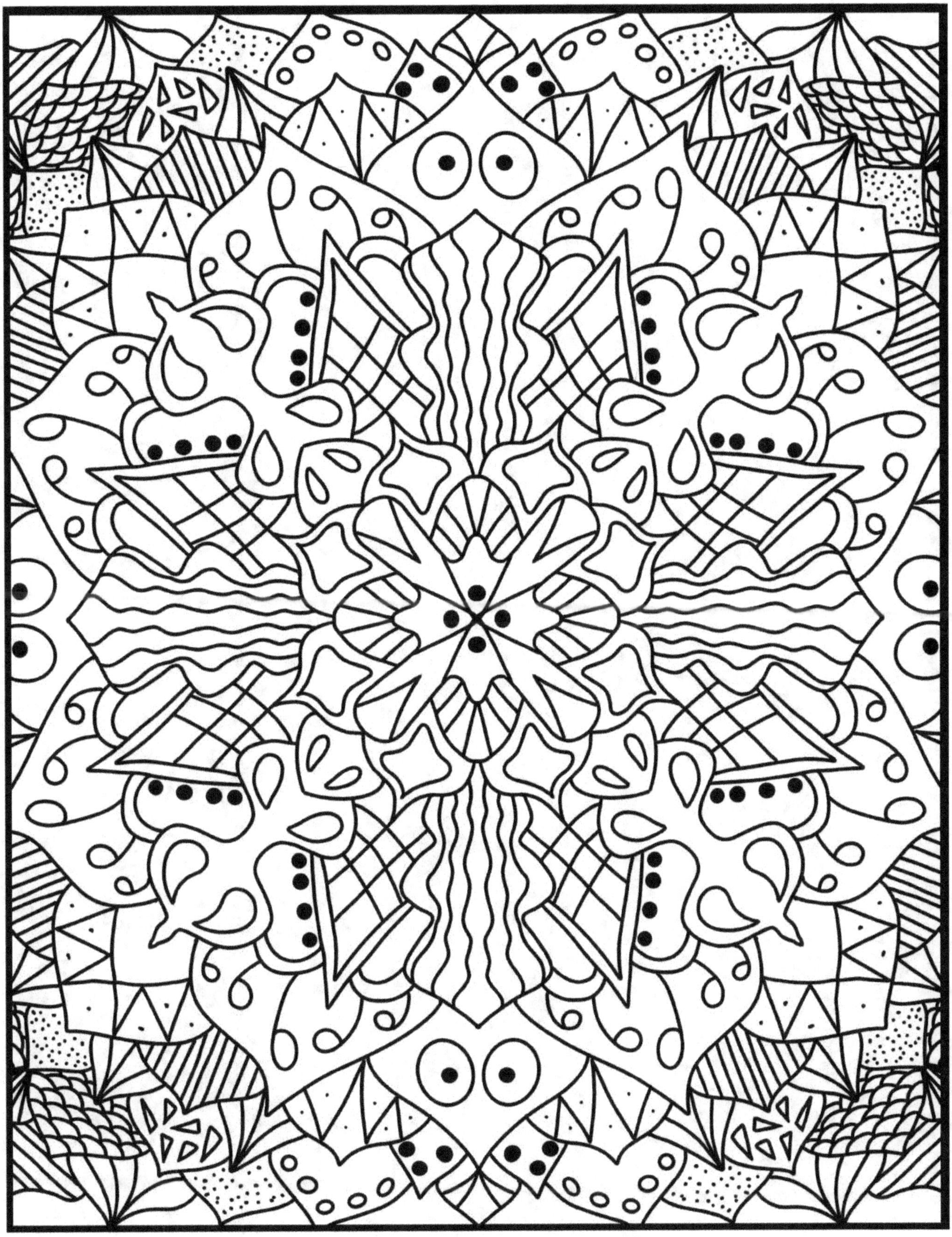

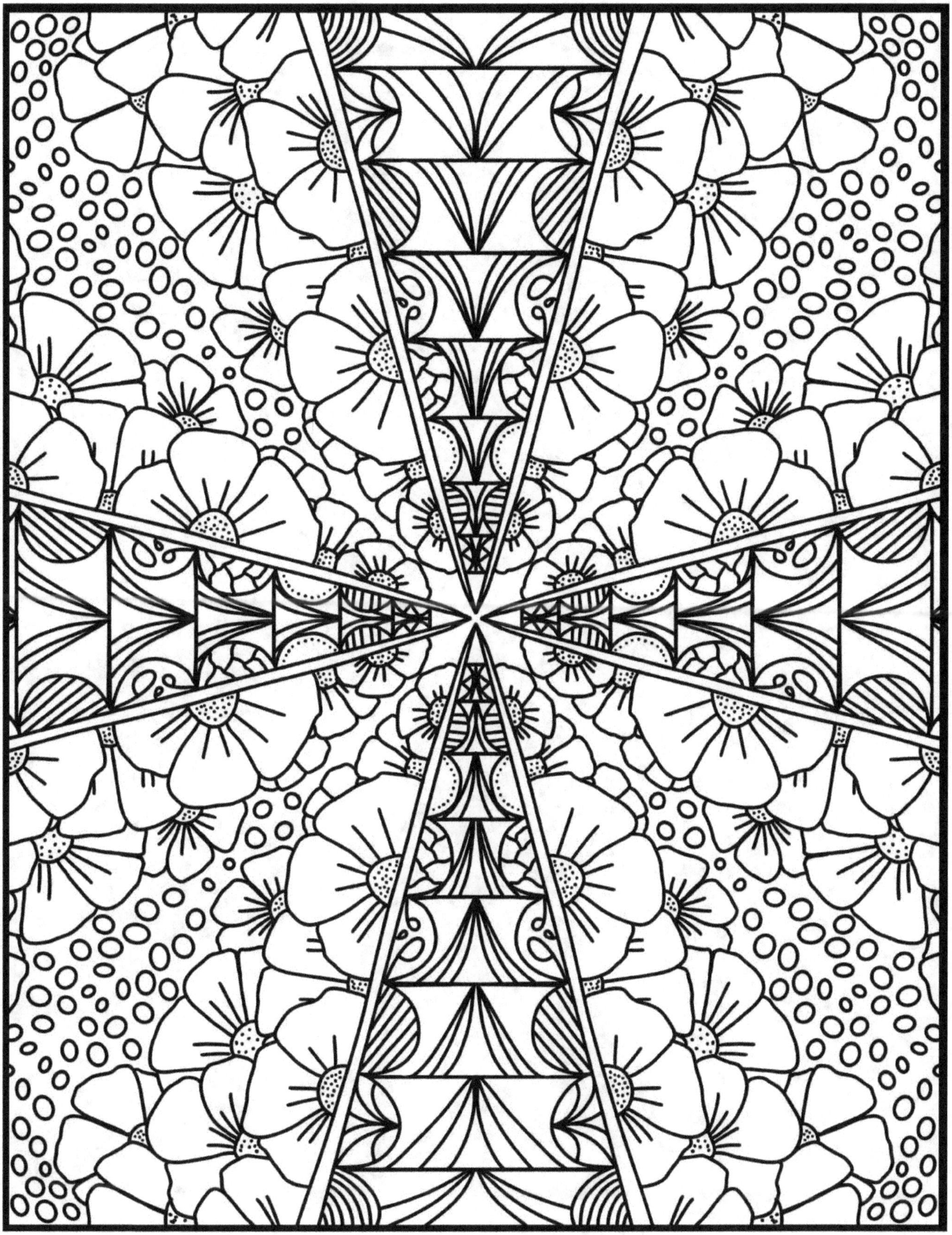

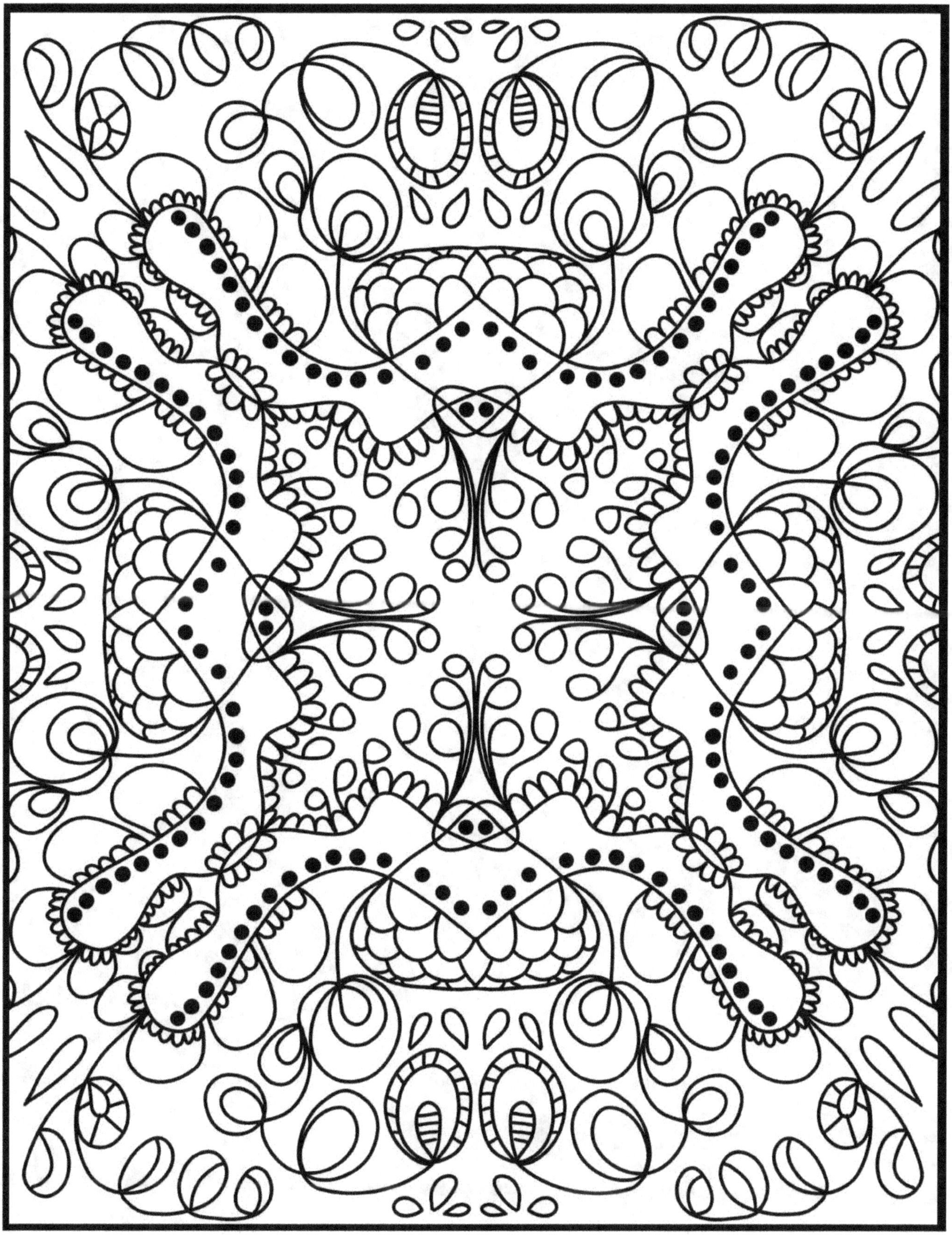

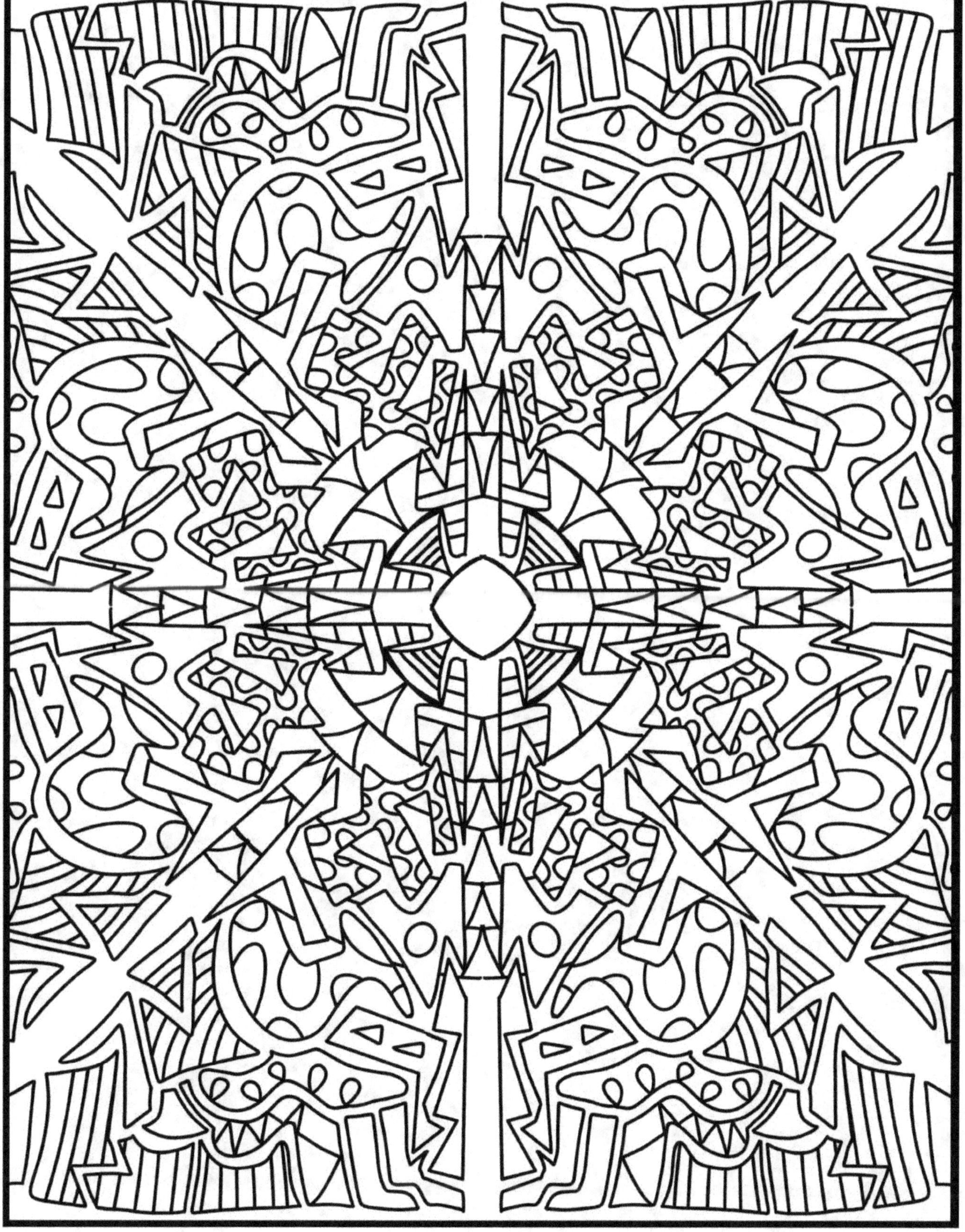

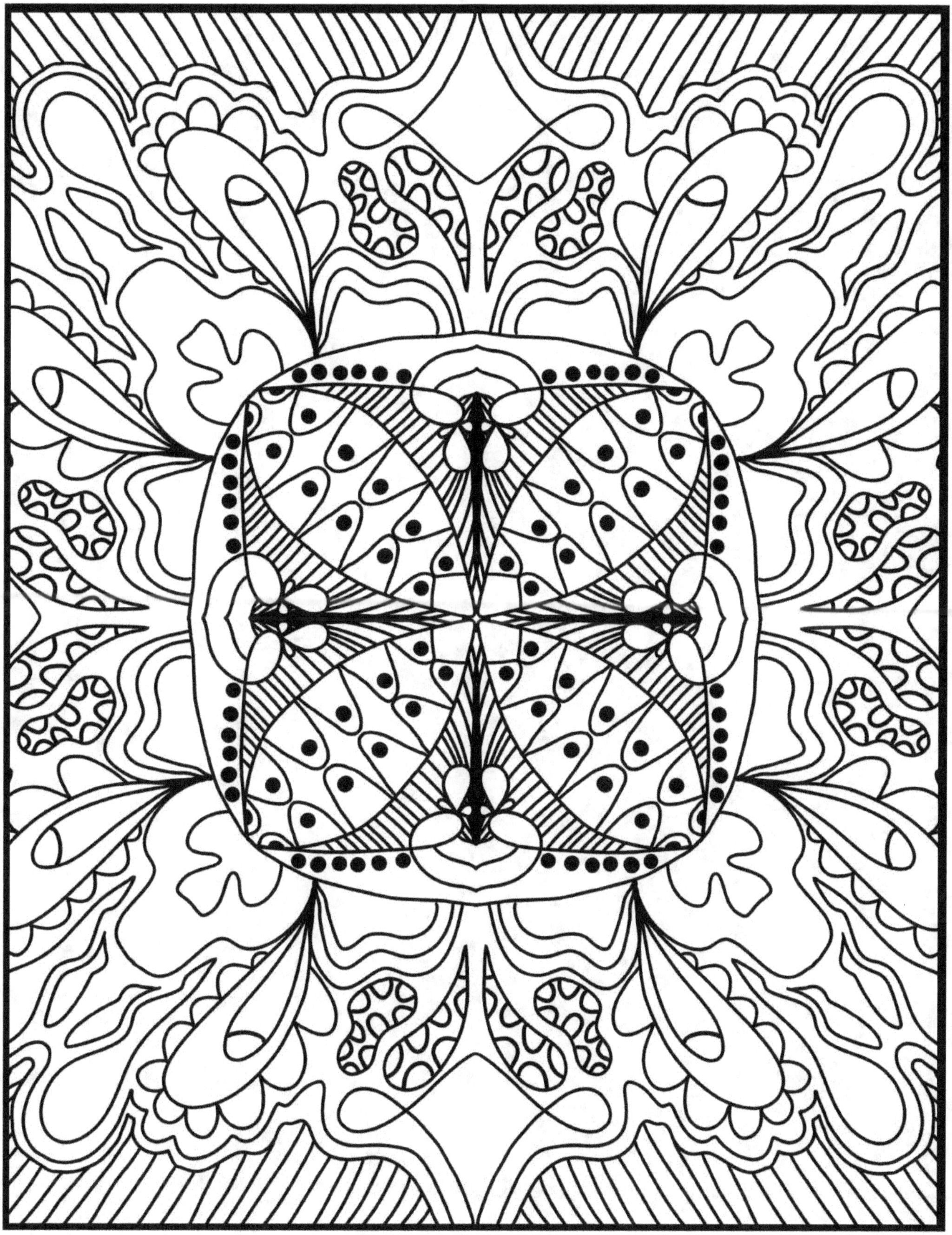

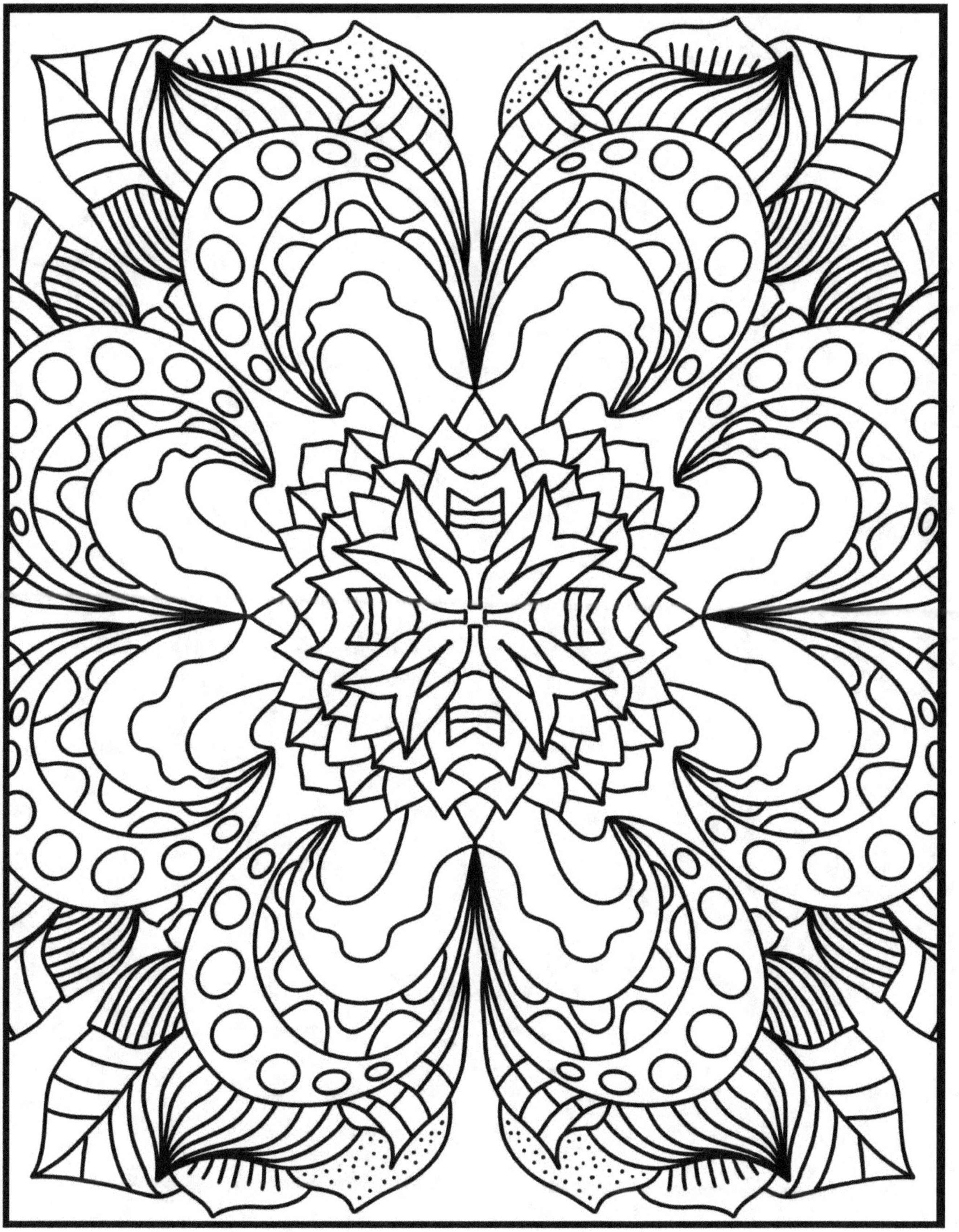

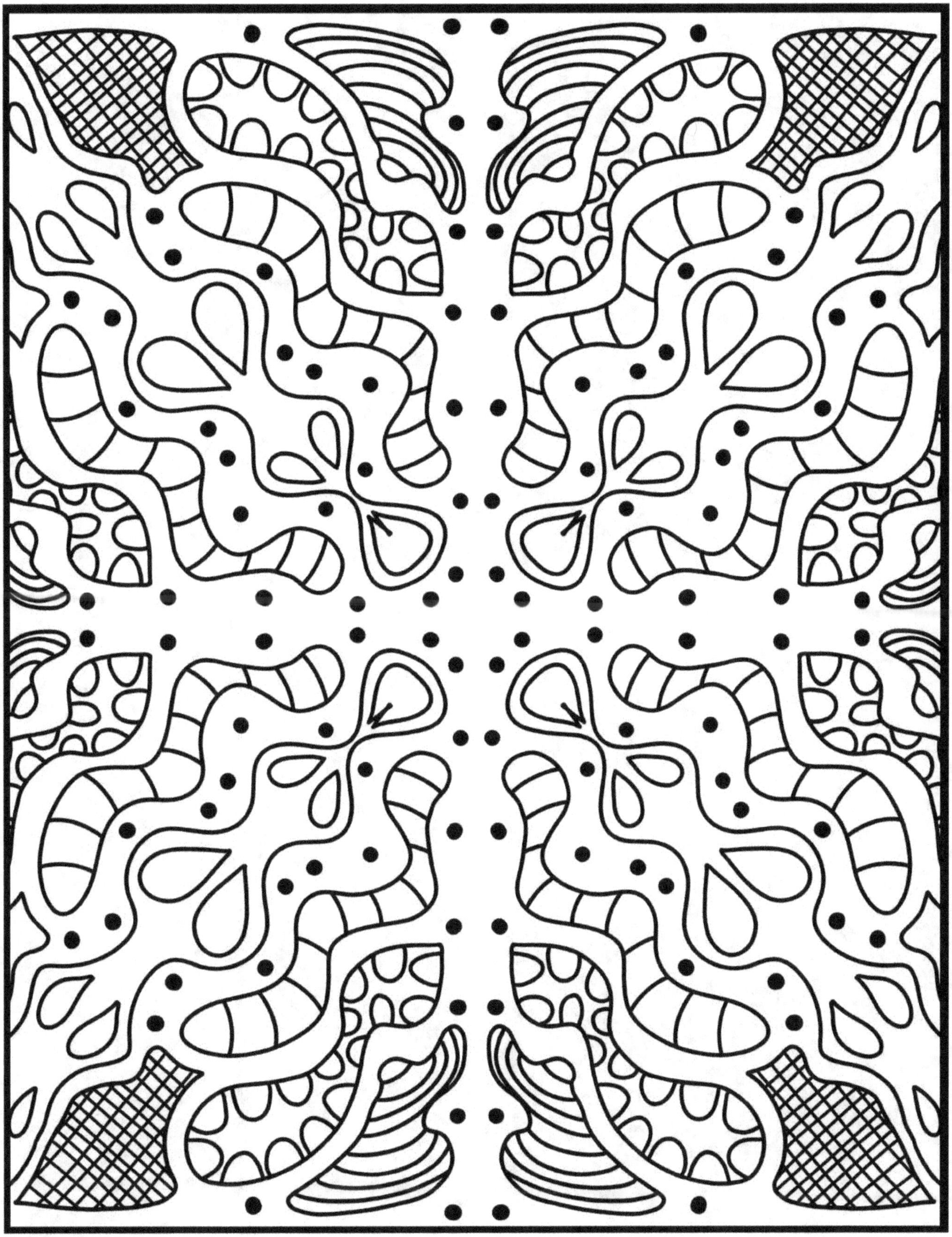

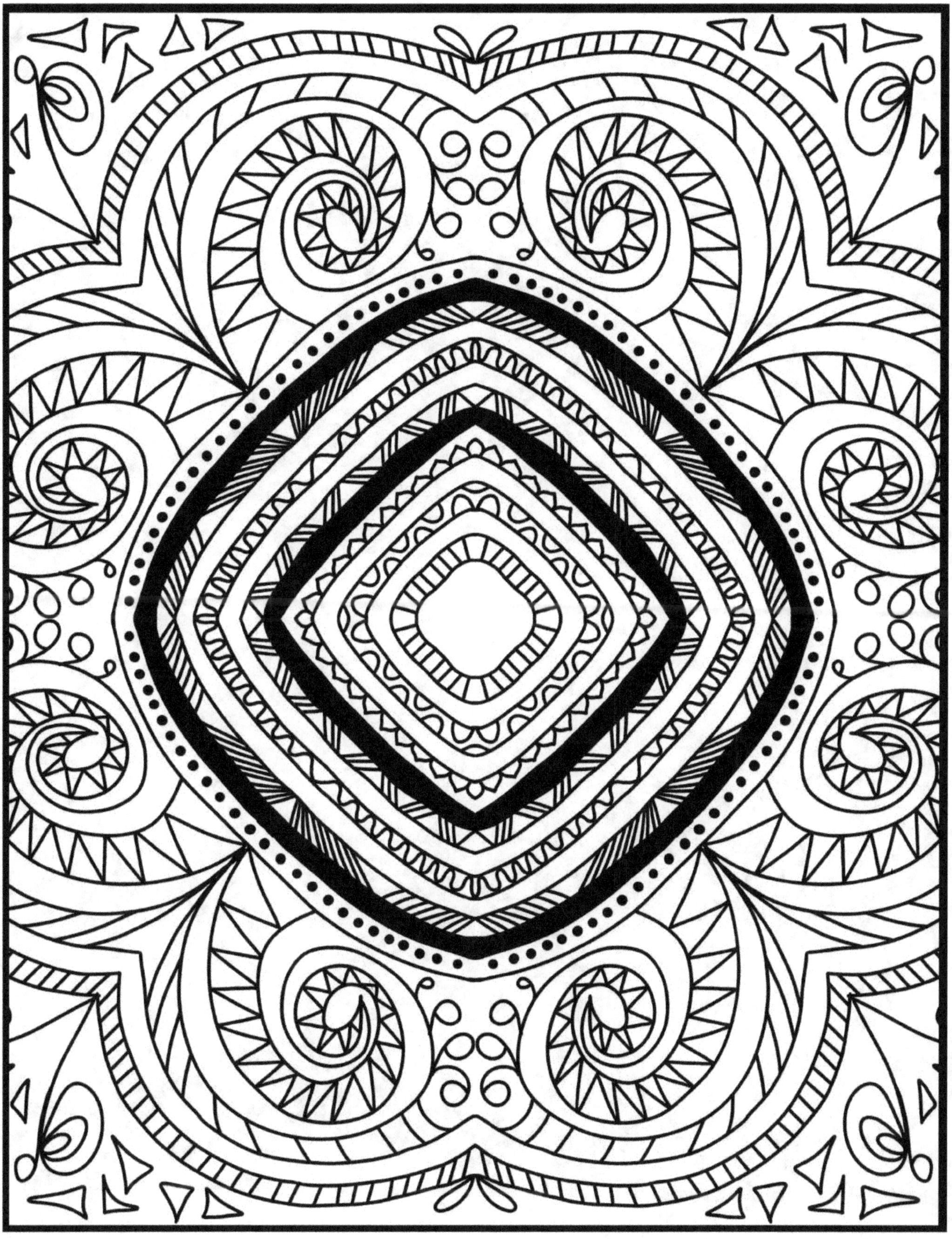

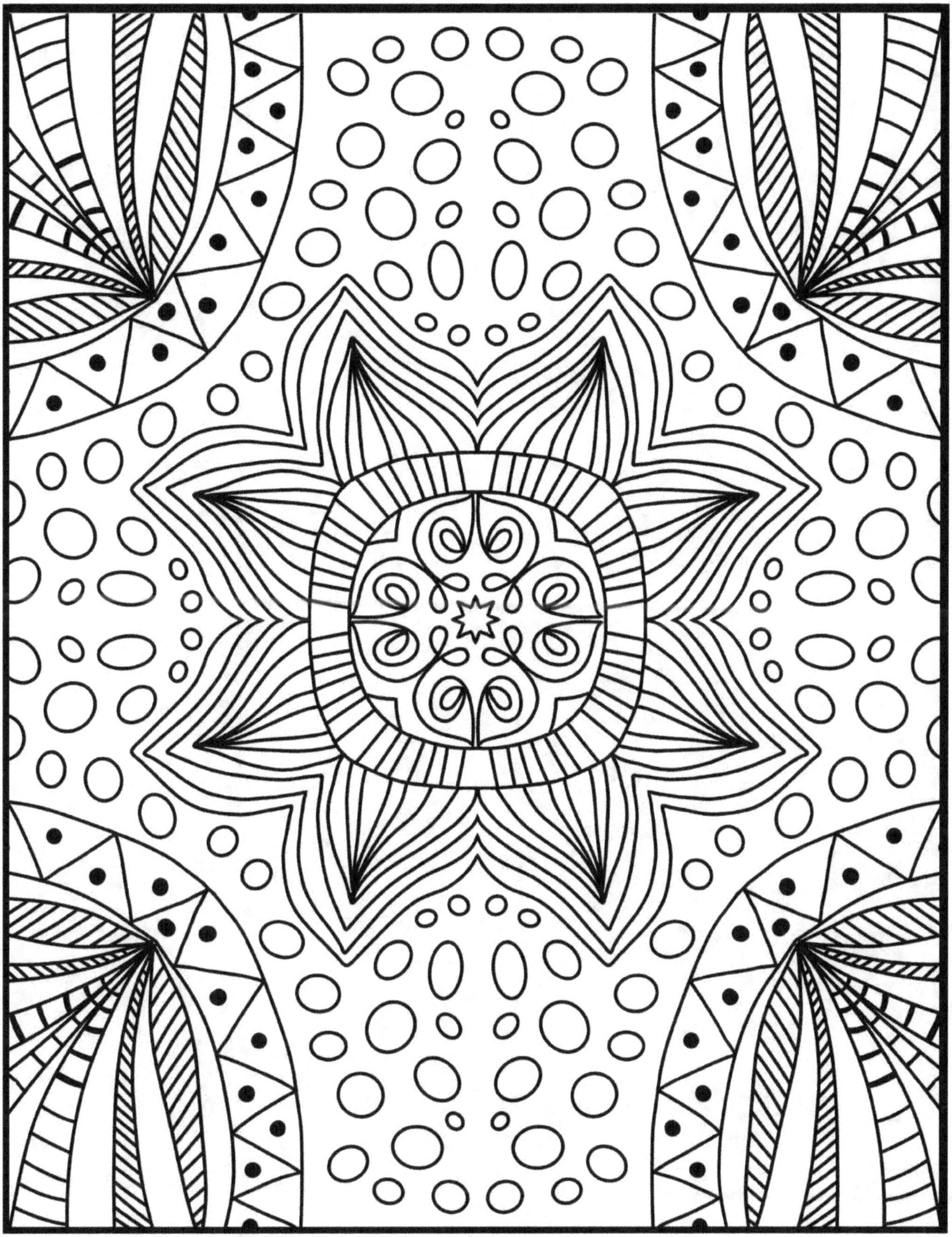

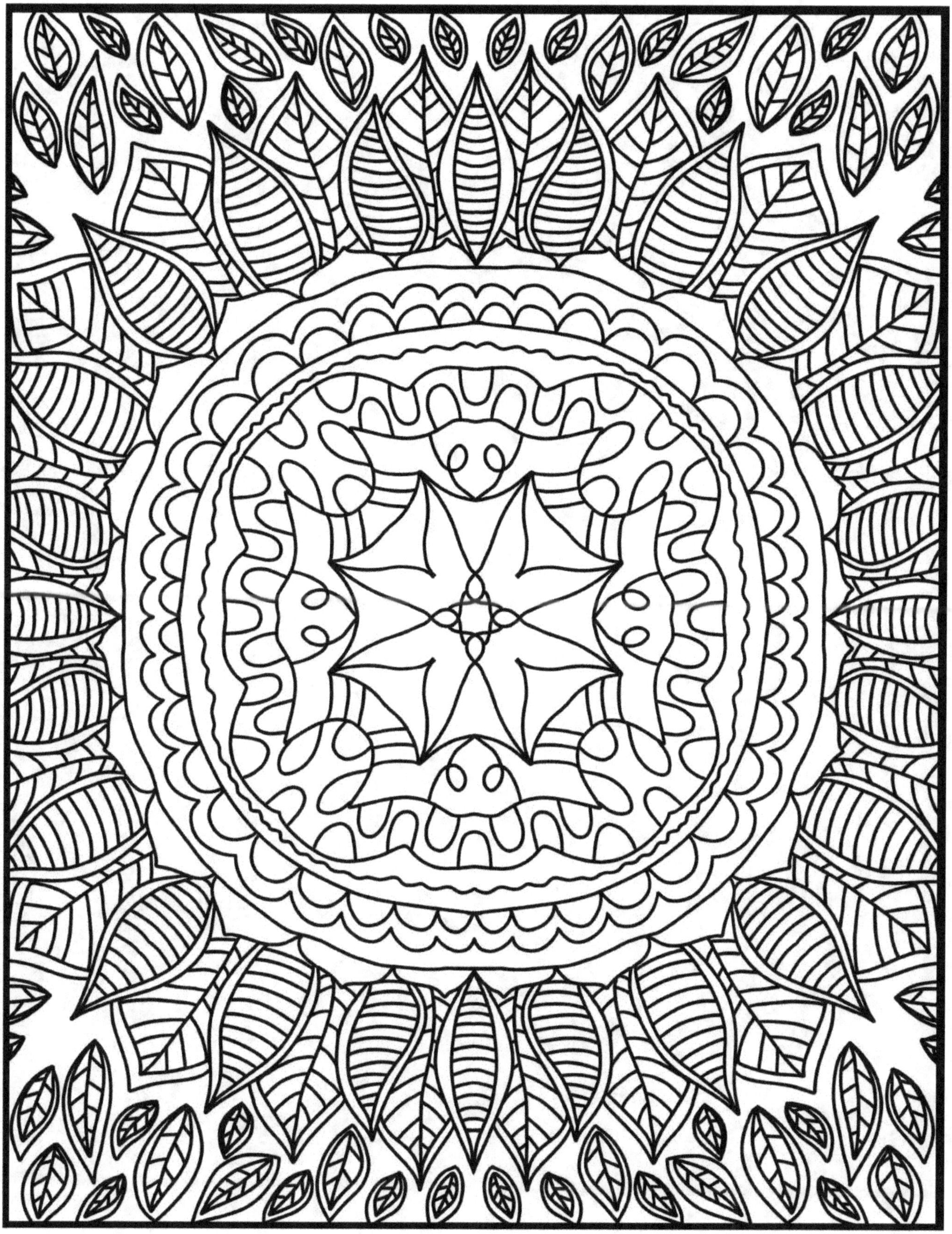

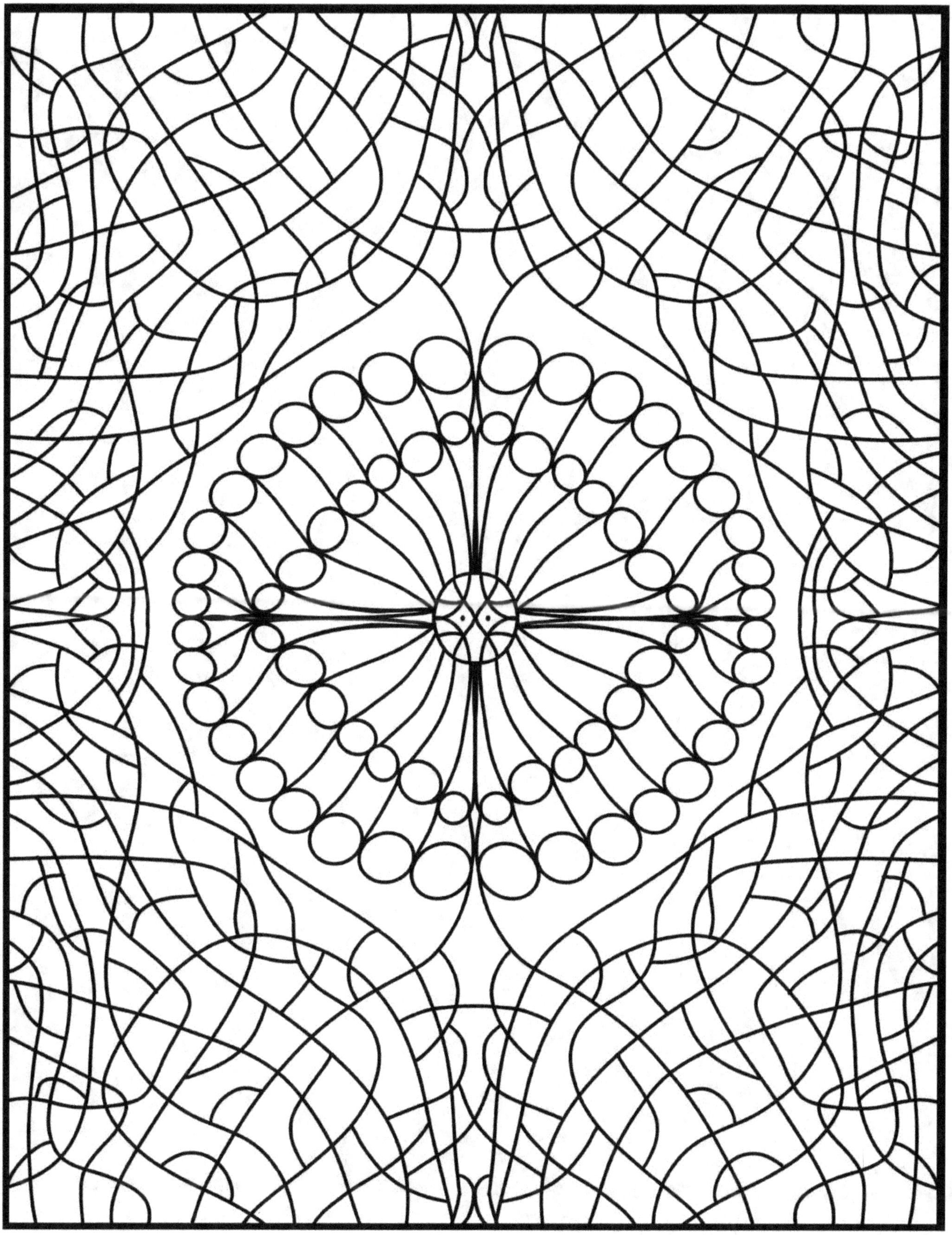

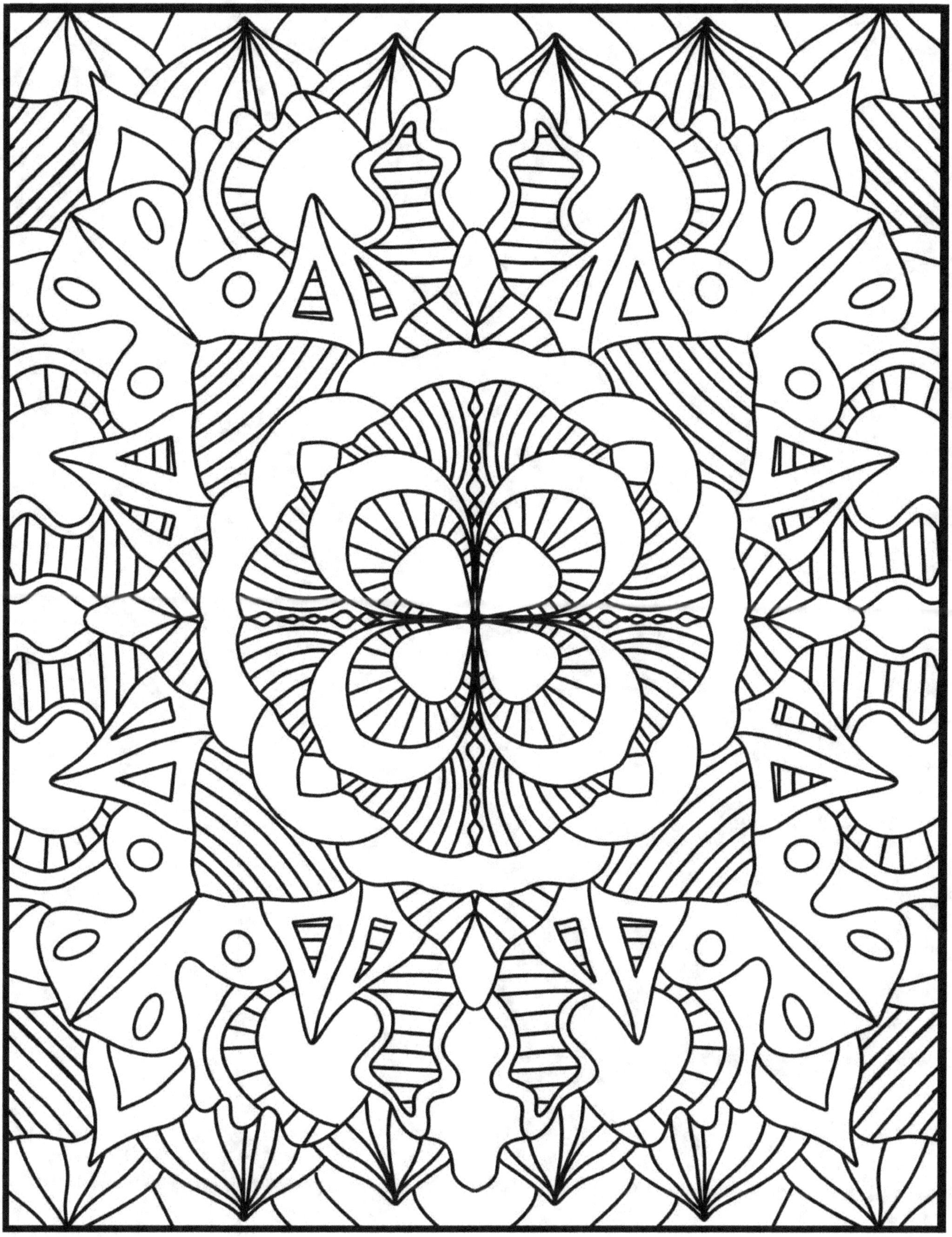

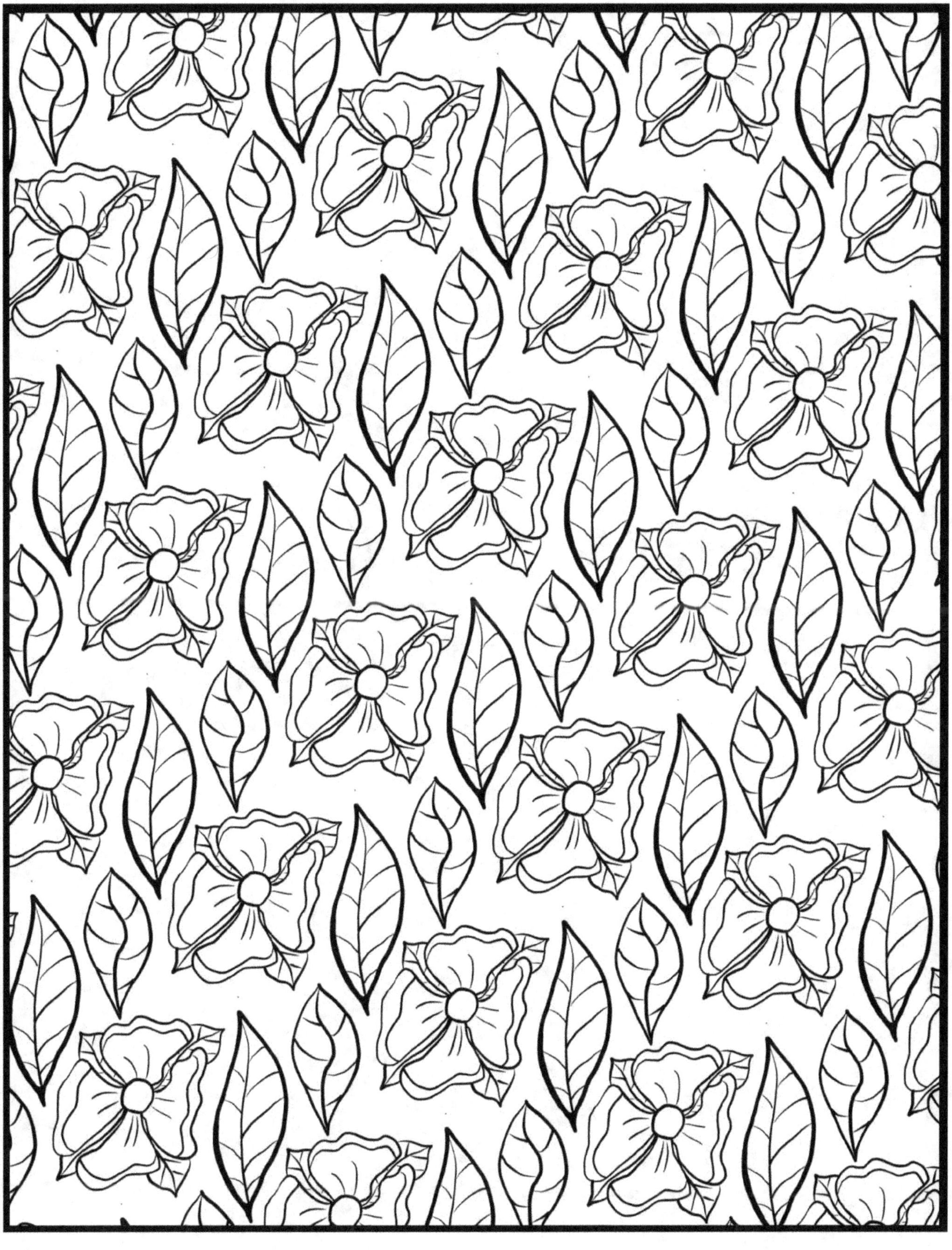

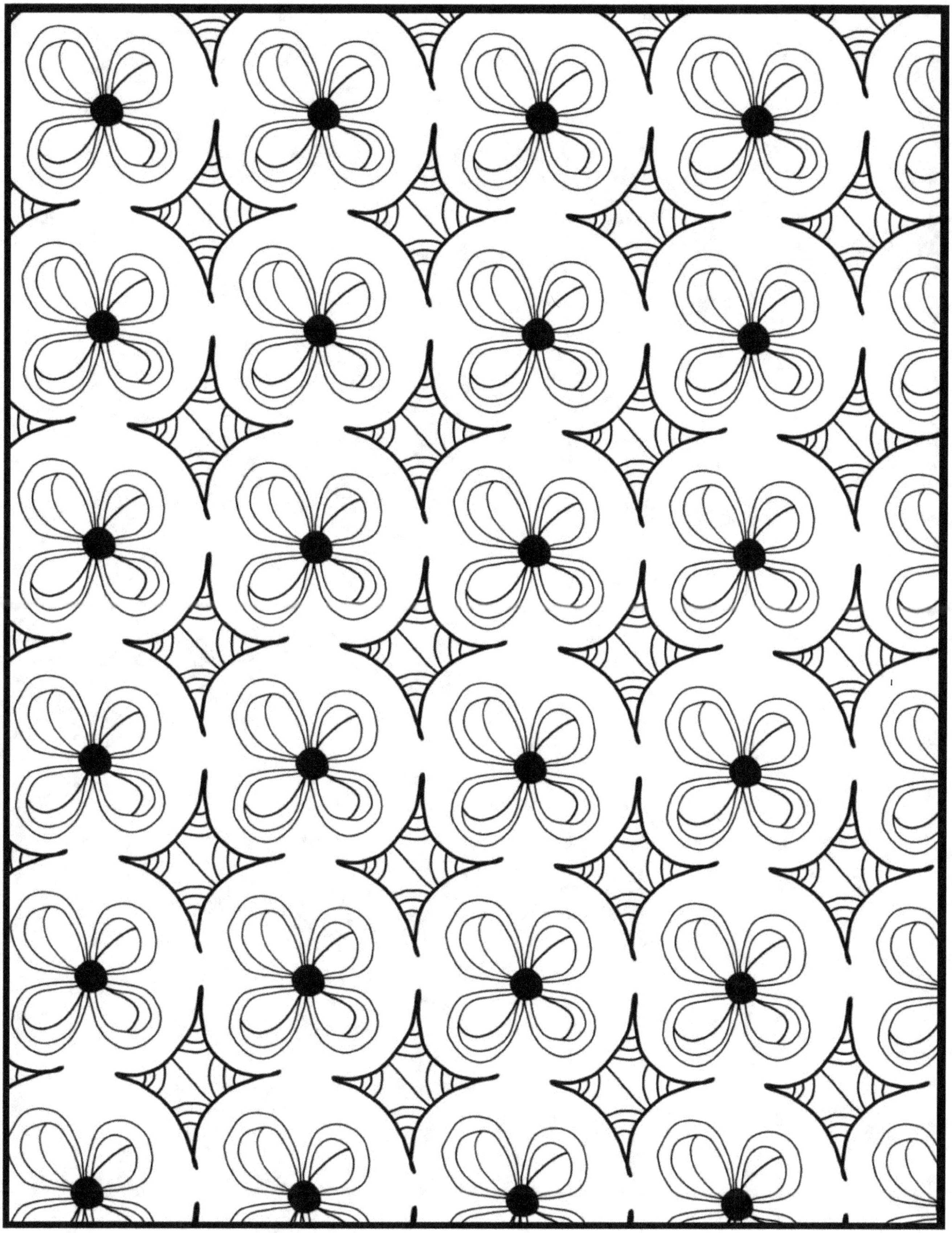

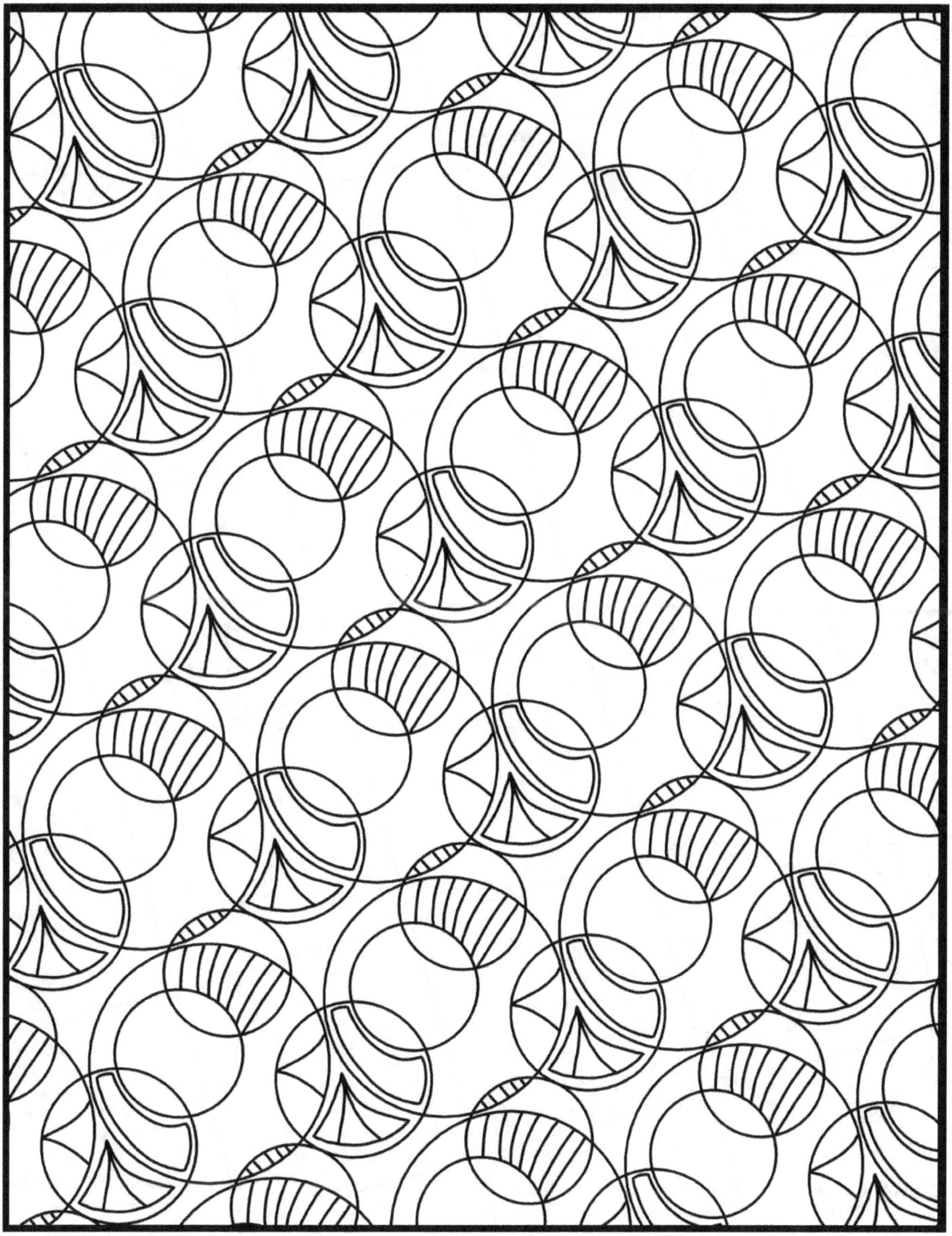

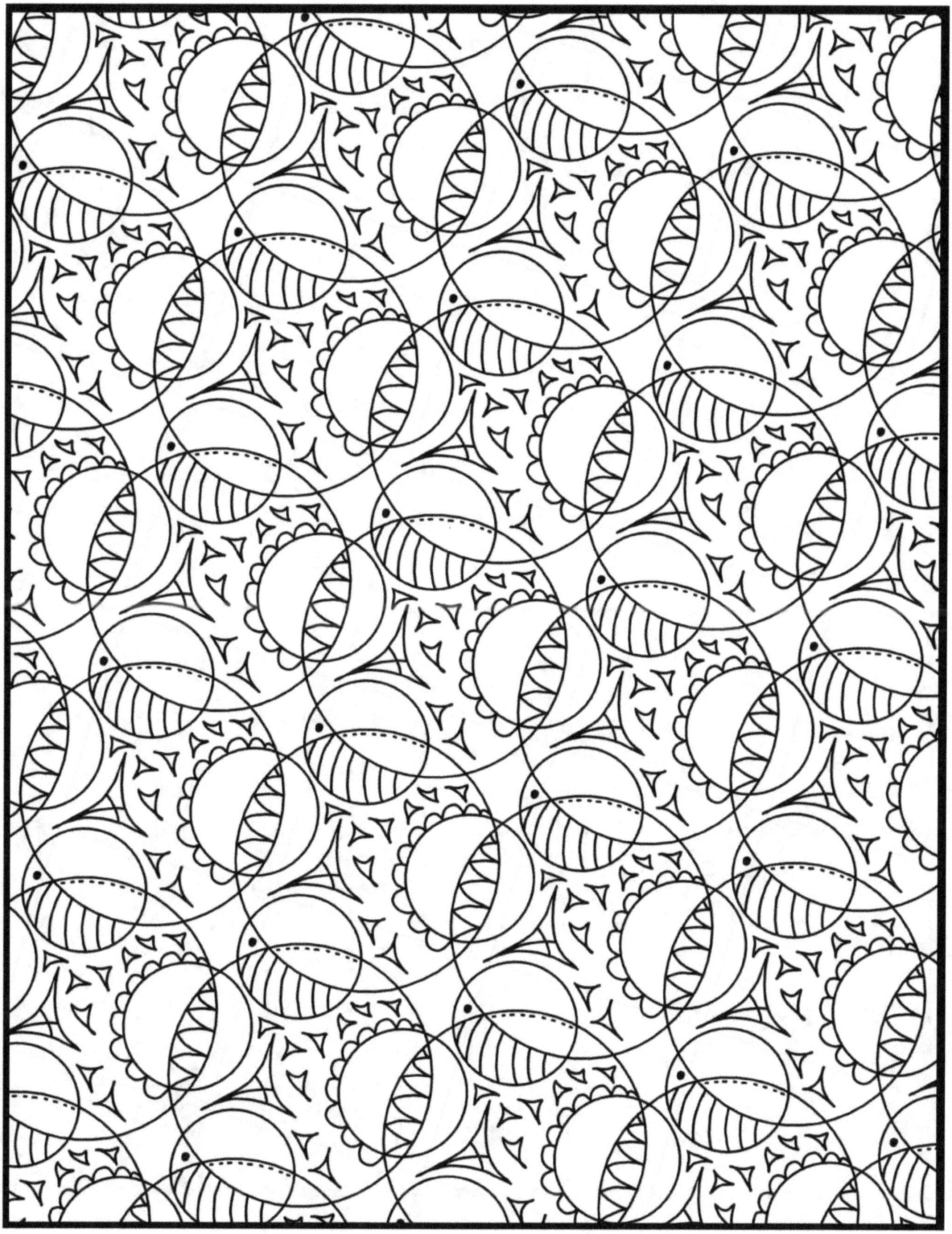

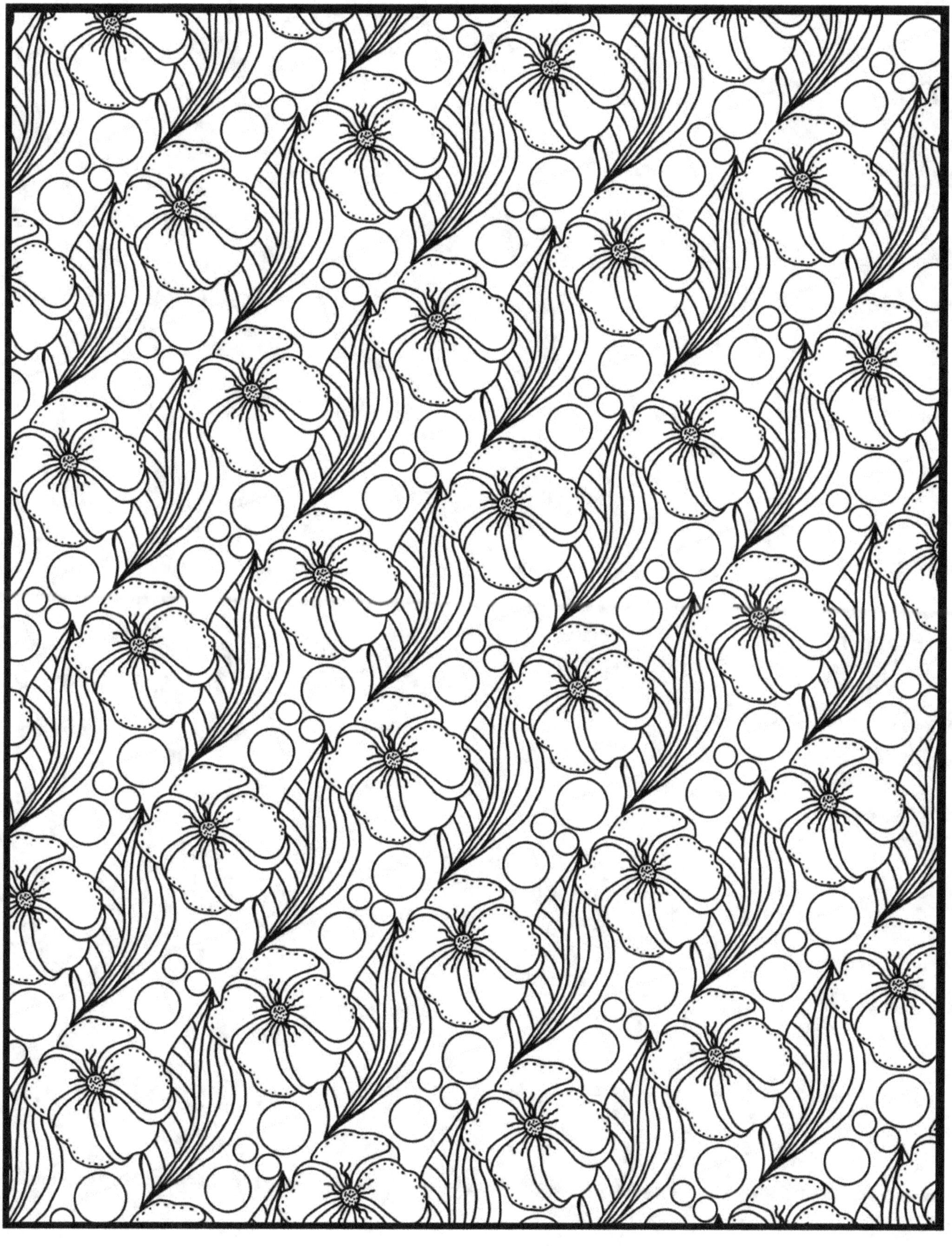

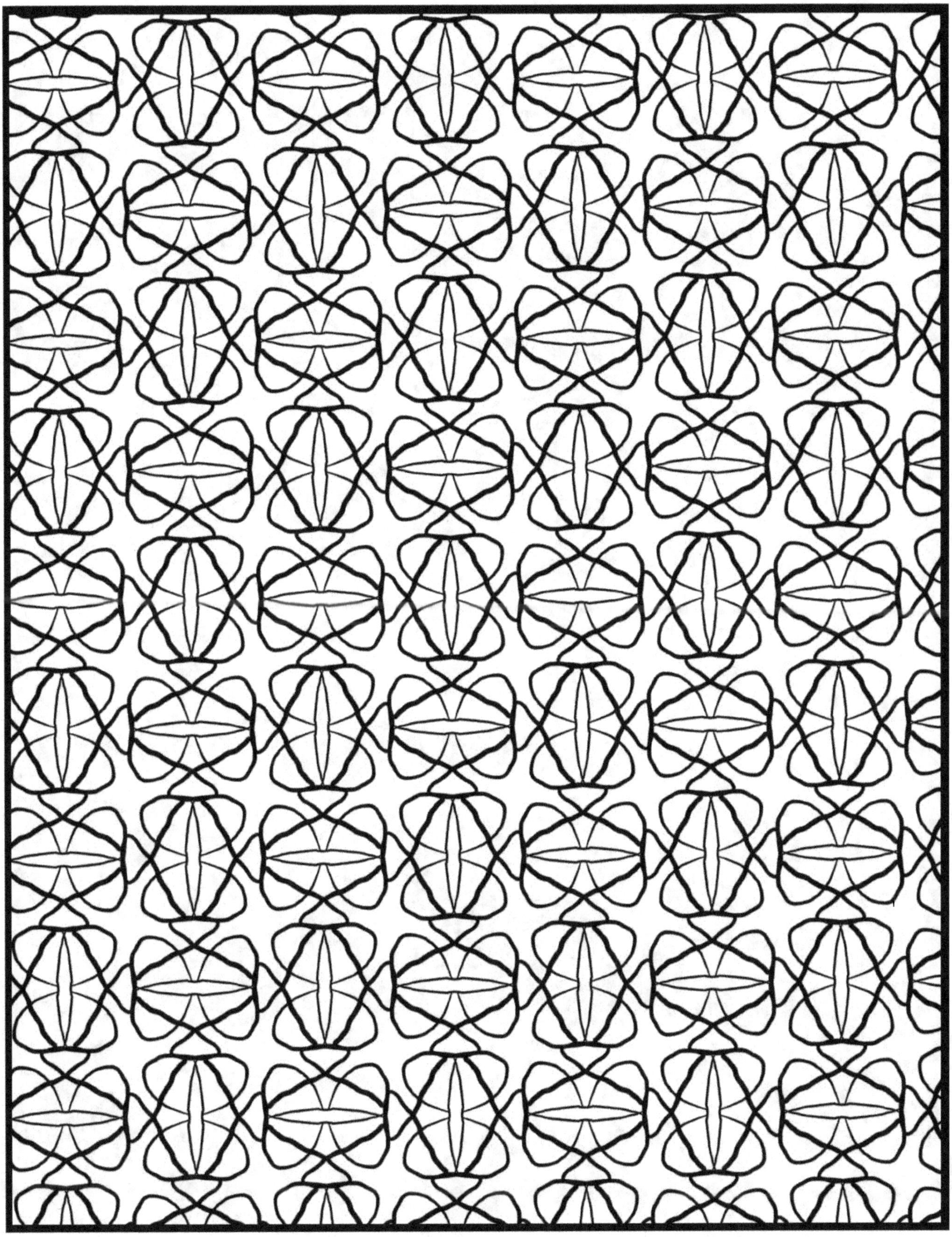

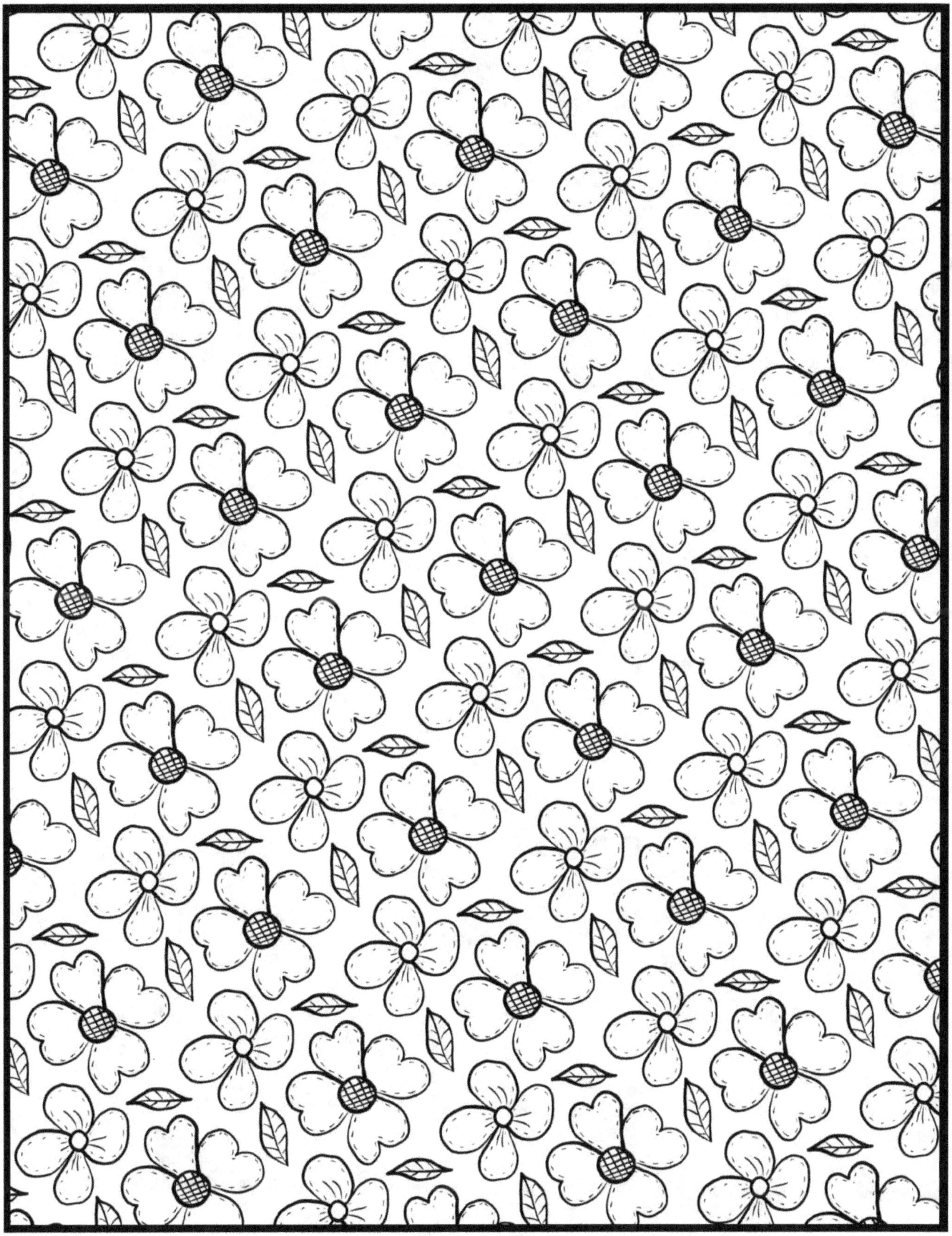

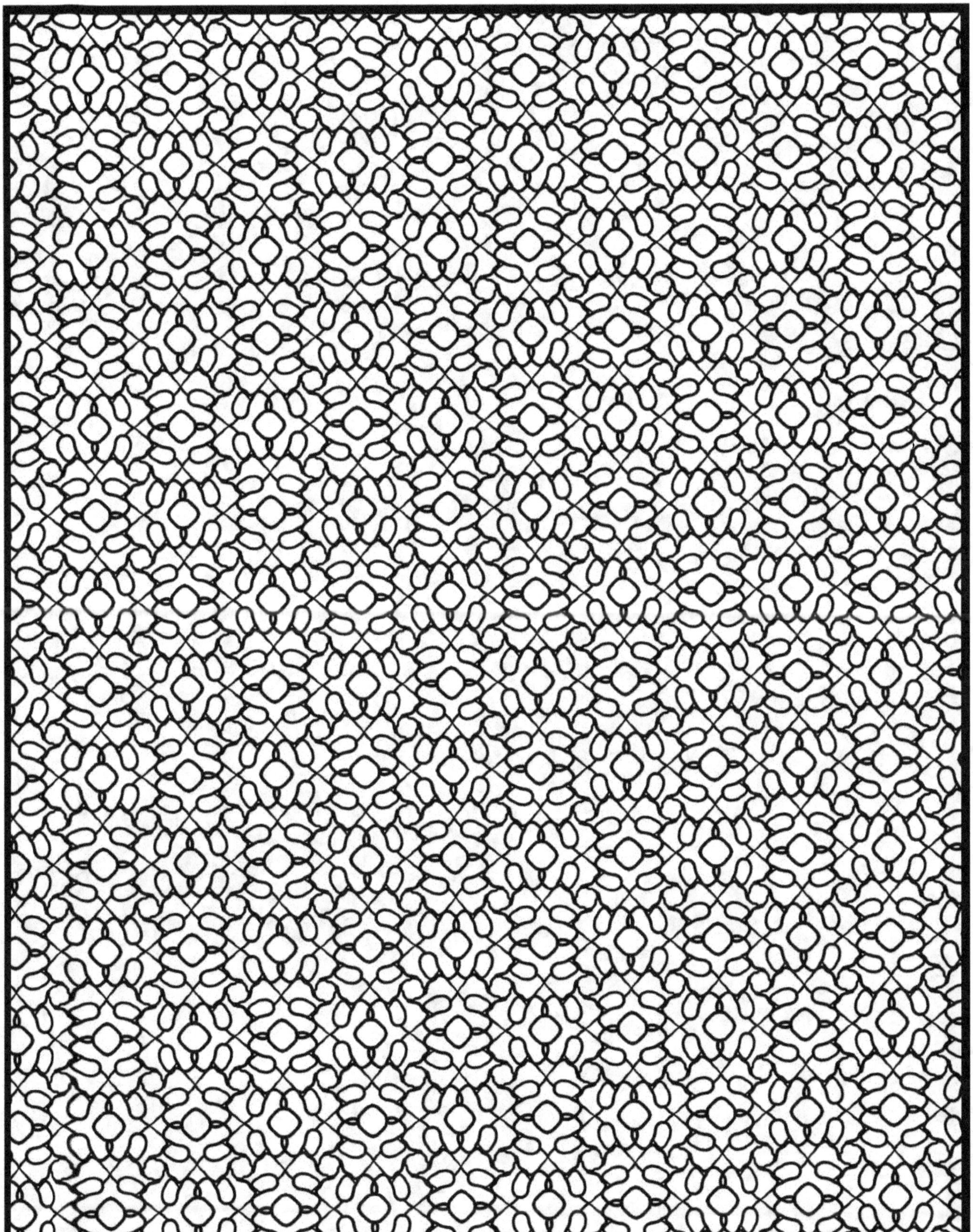

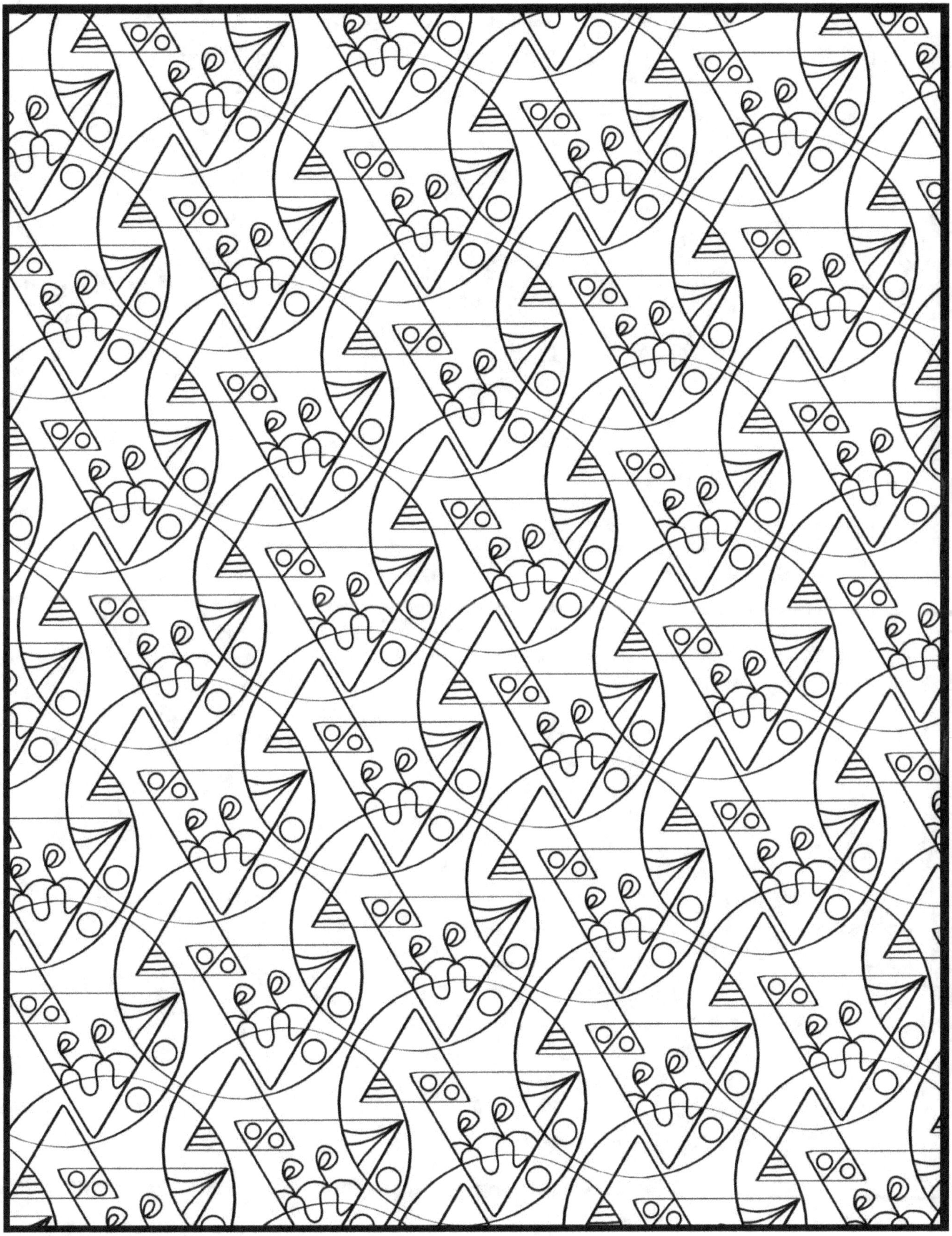

www.ingramcontent.com/pod-product-compliance
Lightning Source LLC
Chambersburg PA
CBHW081533220526
45467CB00010B/3163
* 9 7 9 8 6 9 4 5 1 5 2 5 2 *